How the Economy Works

How the Economy Works

Confidence, Crashes and Self-Fulfilling Prophecies

ROGER E. A. FARMER

OXFORD
UNIVERSITY PRESS
2010

OXFORD
UNIVERSITY PRESS

Oxford University Press, Inc., publishes works that further
Oxford University's objective of excellence
in research, scholarship, and education.

Oxford   New York
Auckland   Cape Town   Dar es Salaam   Hong Kong   Karachi
Kuala Lumpur   Madrid   Melbourne   Mexico City   Nairobi
New Delhi   Shanghai   Taipei   Toronto

With offices in
Argentina   Austria   Brazil   Chile   Czech Republic   France   Greece
Guatemala   Hungary   Italy   Japan   Poland   Portugal   Singapore
South Korea   Switzerland   Thailand   Turkey   Ukraine   Vietnam

Copyright © 2010 by Oxford University Press, Inc.

Published by Oxford University Press, Inc.
198 Madison Avenue, New York, NY 10016

www.oup.com

Oxford is a registered trademark of Oxford University Press.

Library of Congress Cataloging-in-Publication Data
Farmer, Roger E. A.
How the economy works : confidence, crashes and self-fulfilling prophecies / Roger E. A. Farmer.
    p. cm.
Includes bibliographical references and index.
ISBN 978-0-19-539791-8
1. Free enterprise.   2. Monetary policy.   3. Economic policy.
I. Title.
HB95.F37 2010
339—dc22   2009032289

9 8 7 6 5 4 3 2 1

Printed in the United States of America
on acid-free paper

Contents

Preface

Macroeconomics deals with unemployment, inflation, and interest rates: how they are connected and how they are influenced by government monetary and fiscal policy. *How the Economy Works* provides a verbal account of macroeconomics aimed at the general reader. I explain the difference between two main approaches, classical and Keynesian, and I show how they have influenced the policy debate that developed in the wake of the world financial crisis that began in the fall of 2007, with the fall of Northern Rock in the UK, and that exploded into a worldwide catastrophe, with the failure of Lehman Brothers in the United States in the fall of 2008.

But that is not all. This book provides much more than an explanation of existing ideas. It introduces and explains some brand-new ideas that go beyond classical and Keynesian economics. I provide a fresh approach to the prevention of future financial crises and I offer practical policy solutions based on a coherent scientific foundation. The technical and mathematical details are explained elsewhere.[1] This book is for you, the general reader, who wants to make sense of it all.

Why is there so much disagreement among journalists, politicians, and academic economists over the causes of recessions? What went wrong in 2008, and how can we fix it? Who was Keynes, and why are his ideas relevant today? What is the role of the Federal Reserve System, the Bank of England, and the European Central Bank, and how do they affect your life? Does it really make sense for governments around the world to spend hundreds of billions of taxpayer dollars, pounds, and euros that they don't have? In this book, I answer all of these questions and I illustrate the answers with examples. To understand the 2008 financial crisis, it helps to understand what the main protagonists think and how they arrived at their views. The history of the twentieth century is the history of a struggle of ideas between classical and Keynesian economists that continues to this day. Broadly speaking, there were two transformative events in the twentieth century, each of which led to a revolution in thought. These were the Great Depression of the 1930s and stagflation in the 1970s. Before 1930, most economists were classical. Between 1930 and 1970, Keynesian thought was in the ascendancy, and from 1970 to the present day, there was a revival of classical thought ushered in by a set of new ideas called the rational expectations revolution. With the financial crisis of 2008, we have arrived at a third turning point that demands a new approach. By combining the best ideas of the rational expectations revolution with the most important insights from Keynes, I show in this book where we should go from here.

One goal of this book is to provide a lightening tour of the history of economic thought from 1776 to the present day. I am painfully aware that this tour is incomplete. Many key players are missing and the ideas of others have been simplified. To those readers who recognize these deficiencies, I plead guilty. In my own defense, I can say only that to do justice to my intellectual predecessors would take a much larger book than this one. A second goal is to present a new theory that is intelligible to the layperson, but at the same time detailed enough for an academic economist to see where I disagree with existing economic theory and how it needs to be changed. I'm not sure when the word *wonkish* arrived in the English language, but it is surely an apt description of some chapters of this book, particularly chapter 7, which is the most wonkish of the lot. I left this chapter in the book even though, after 12 rewrites, it still retains an aura of impenetrability. It is there for the academic economist or the serious general reader who is interested in the arcane question of what *exactly* goes wrong with the market economy and why unemployment persists. I take some solace in the words of Albert Einstein, who said "everything should be made as simple as possible, but no simpler."

Many people have helped me with this book. I want to thank my colleagues and students at UCLA—Andy Atkeson, Amy Brown, Francisco Buera, Ariel Burstein, Anton Cheremukhin, Hal Cole, Matthias Doepke, Corey Garriott, Gary Hansen, Christian Hellwig, Andrew Hollenhorst, Hugo Hopenhayn, Masanori Kashiwagi, Kei Kawakami, Hanno Lustig, Lee Ohanian, Paulina Restrepo, Hao Shi, Jonathan Vogel, Pierre-Olivier Weill, and Mark Wright. I have been privileged to present the ideas in this book at seminars and workshops throughout the world and to receive the feedback of many of my colleagues who have provided invaluable input. Riccardo DiCecio from the St. Louis Fed, Marco Guerrazzi of the University of Pisa, and Colin Rogers of the University of Adelaide gave me detailed comments on my ideas. I thank all of them for helping me to weed out mistakes, although I am sure that some remain.

I am grateful to the National Science Foundation, which has supported my research for many years with a series of grants that gave me the freedom to think independently and to develop new ideas. Most recently I was awarded grant #SBR 0720839, which helped to support the research developed in this book. My editor, Terry Vaughn, provided encouragement, support, and an education in how to write for a general audience. I am grateful to Terry and the entire team at Oxford University Press for their faith in and support of the project.

Last, but by no means least, I owe a huge debt to my son, Leland, and my wife, Roxanne, for their love and unfaltering encouragement. Roxanne read several drafts of the manuscript, made suggestions for improvement, and helped me to write more clearly and avoid jargon. To the extent that I have succeeded, she deserves the credit.

CHAPTER 1

Introduction

If economists could manage to get themselves thought of as humble,
competent people on a level with dentists, that would be splendid.
—John Maynard Keynes (1931, p. 373 of the 1963
Norton edition)

THE COLLAPSE OF NORTHERN ROCK

In September 2007, I attended a conference at the Bank
of England. The topic was "The Great Moderation." This
is the name given by economists to the fact that the postwar global financial system displayed greater stability in the
period after 1980 than before. From 1951 through 1979,
inflation, interest rates, and unemployment were high and
volatile. After 1980, they all fell and began to display more
moderate fluctuations from month to month. The world
had changed. But why?

Economists from around the globe met in London in
a self-congratulatory mood. Our task was to decide if the
remarkable improvement in worldwide economic fortunes
was due to new technology, a better understanding of monetary policy by economists and central bankers, or plain
good luck. Many of the papers presented at the conference argued that central bankers were doing a much better job through a new policy, inflation targeting, and that
new-Keynesian monetary theory, developed by academic

economists, had led to improved global financial stability. How wrong we were.

On the evening of September 13, the final day of the conference, we convened for dinner in the Court Room of the Bank. The dinner was to be hosted by the governor, Mervyn King, who was unaccountably delayed. Charlie Bean, who was then research director of the Bank, gave the welcoming address. At my table, there were five academics plus Rachel Lomax, one of two deputy governors. It was a spectacular dinner. The staff of the Bank wear red waistcoats and pink top coats, and the Court Room of the Bank is an architectural jewel and one of the few surviving rooms from architect John Soane's original 1814 building, most of which was rebuilt in 1925. I had a lively discussion with Rachel Lomax, which was frequently punctuated by messages from men in pink coats who would call her away temporarily to take care of urgent business. Mervyn King never appeared. I learned the next day that I had been present during negotiations for the first major bank bailout of what was to become the largest financial crisis since the Great Depression.

In 2007, Northern Rock was one of the five largest mortgage lenders in the UK. It had begun life as a building society, a peculiarly British cooperative institution that ploughed back all profits to its members. Traditionally, banks and building societies in the UK borrowed money from local savers. They took this money and lent it to local borrowers in the form of mortgages that were secured by residential property. The bank manager knew the customers and had a personal relationship with all of his clients. The building societies were owned by the savers, and any profits they made through spreads on lending and borrowing rates were returned to savers as dividends.

In the 1990s, Northern Rock was allowed by the government to convert itself into a profit-making institution and to sell shares on the stock exchange. In the early years of the new millennium, Northern Rock and other commercial banks began to make riskier loans and to borrow from each other on a short-term basis to provide the capital for their mortgages. Northern Rock began to provide mortgages worth 125% of the value of homes. Since it had a relatively small amount of deposits from savers, it relied instead on the ability to borrow money cheaply on the London Interbank Market to finance its loans.

The rate at which banks borrow and lend to each other is called LIBOR, the London Interbank Offered Rate. In August 2007, the LIBOR began to climb steeply and Northern Rock's business model became unsustainable. It was forced to ask the Bank of England for emergency funds, and in February 2008, Northern Rock became the first of many world financial institutions to be owned, wholly or in part, by the taxpayer. Shortly following the fall of Northern Rock, the global financial system underwent a meltdown that hadn't been seen since the 1930s. This book is about how we got to that point and what we can do in the future to prevent it from happening again.

CLASSICAL AND KEYNESIAN ECONOMICS

There is a major disagreement between two groups of economists about how the economy works. On one side, there are *classical economists* such as Eugene Fama of the University of Chicago, who believe that unregulated markets are inherently self-stabilizing and that government intervention often does more harm than good. On the other side, there are *Keynesian economists* such as the Nobel Laureate and *New York Times* columnist Paul Krugman, who believe that the market system needs a little help sometimes.

In the 1980s, the U.S. presidency under Ronald Reagan and the UK government under Margaret Thatcher were strongly influenced by classical economics. A leading exponent of classical ideas was Friedrich Hayek, an Austrian intellectual who fled Hitler's Germany to teach at the London School of Economics. In 1944, he published an influential book, *The Road to Serfdom*, which argued that the trend toward collectivization occurring throughout the West in the 1940s was incompatible with democracy.[1] Hayek was a strong opponent of all forms of socialism and his ideas were an important influence on Margaret Thatcher.[2] Hayek's philosophy is aptly summarized by Ronald Reagan's famous quip: "The nine most terrifying words in the English language are: 'I'm from the government and I'm here to help.'"

In contrast to the economics of Reagan and Thatcher, the Obama administration of 2009 is strongly influenced by the ideas of John Maynard Keynes, a British economist who wrote a famous book in 1936, *The General Theory of Employment, Interest and Money*. In it, he developed a completely new theory of how the economy works. Keynes argued that the Great Depression occurred because firms were not spending enough on factories and machines and that this lack of private investment expenditure should be replaced by government expenditure that was to be financed by borrowing. His arguments were responsible for the fact that government in the United States currently accounts for nearly one-third of the entire economy.

Hayek was a champion of individual freedom and a fierce opponent of socialism. He believed that government intervention in markets more often does more harm than good. In contrast, Keynes thought that markets must be regulated to help them work better. For him, government intervention is like adding oil to a squeaky wheel. In 2007, the debate between classical and Keynesian economics reemerged with a vengeance and battles over government's role were once more fought in the pages of the *Wall Street Journal* and the *New York Times*. What are the battles? Who are the protagonists? Who is right?

THE SIZE OF GOVERNMENT

Should government be big or should it be small? Should government intervene in markets sometimes or should it always let markets operate freely? Although these are distinct questions, they are often confounded. The first relates to which goods and services should be provided by the free market and which by the government. The second relates to the rules under which the free market will operate.

As a society, we must choose whether to provide publicly funded pension systems. We must decide whether education is to be provided by the state or by the free market. And we must decide whether health care is to be freely provided to all and, if so, how much of it to provide. These are all questions about the size and scope of government.

Given that some services are to be provided by the market, what laws should govern interactions among citizens in market transactions? When a firm goes bankrupt, how should we divide its assets among different types of creditors? Should government prevent some mergers on the grounds that a very large company can restrict competition? Should all prices be chosen freely by the market, or are there some prices that must be controlled through government intervention? These are all questions about the rules under which the free market should operate.

Although there are no right answers to these questions, there are important principles that should govern our choices. History has shown us that free market economies can provide faster growth and higher living standards than planned economies. There was a reason for the fall of the Berlin Wall in 1989 and for the decision of Communist China to adopt a market system after President Nixon's visit to China in 1972. Capitalism is the single most successful engine of growth in human history. It is responsible for lifting more people from starvation and misery than any known alternative. But capitalism is not a monolithic concept; it comes in different forms and it cannot exist without a well-defined legal code. The question is not whether to regulate capitalism: It is how to regulate it.

EFFICIENT MARKETS

Classical economics today is championed in the United States by economists from the University of Chicago, which boasts five living Nobel Laureates in economics. A leading figure at Chicago is Eugene Fama, known for his work on the efficient market hypothesis. This is the idea that financial markets summarize all of the information that participants need to make quick and efficient decisions. In the 1990s, investment banks began to develop new kinds of financial instruments, called derivatives, that split the payments from business ventures into pieces and allowed market participants to trade different kinds of risk. The theory that traders use to price derivatives was developed by academic financial economists.

As new financial instruments were developed, the banks that created and traded them made huge commissions every time they changed hands. Along with high commissions went enormous compensation packages for traders and executives. Million-dollar bonuses were common and chief executive bonuses were often in the tens of millions of dollars. The record in 2006 was a $53.4 million bonus paid to Goldman Sachs CEO Lloyd Blankfein.[3]

Why were the titans of finance paid so much? According to efficient market theory, the creation of new markets for derivatives was responsible for growth in the real economy. Derivatives markets enable traders to share risk efficiently, and the development of new derivatives markets encouraged firms to engage in profit-making activities that they might otherwise have avoided. As firms made profit, they created jobs, and according to the theory, everybody was a winner. Traders in the financial markets truly believed that, in the new world order, the creation of derivatives had helped to eliminate the adverse effects of risk by sharing it among a larger number of participants.

In the 1990s, regulations governing the financial services industry in the United States were relaxed. Most notably, the 1933 Glass-Steagall Act that had placed a wall between commercial banks and investment banks was repealed in 1999. Deregulation of this kind contributed to the creation of the markets for new and exotic derivatives, and some have argued that deregulation was responsible for the 2007–2008 financial crisis.[4] I find this argument unpersuasive, not least because bubbles and crashes have been with us as long as there have been organized markets.

Regulations such as the Glass-Steagall Act may have contributed to a long period of relative stability after World War II. But active monetary policy by the Bank of England and the Fed in the United States also helped. What is different about the 2008 crisis is not the end of regulation; it is the fact that the interest rate is close to zero and central banks are unable to lower rates further to stimulate the economy. This is exactly what happened in the United States in the 1930s, and it has happened again recently, not just in the United States, but also in Continental Europe and the UK.

The crisis that began in 2007 was preceded by a bubble: a rapid expansion and subsequent collapse of an asset price that is not connected in any obvious way with market fundamentals. Bubbles are common in financial markets and they are often followed by recessions. Earlier examples of bubbles include the Tulip Mania of 1637, the South Sea bubble of 1720, and a series of financial panics in the United States in 1819, 1837, 1857, 1873, and 1893, each of which was similar in character to the Great Depression of the 1930s.

The Tulip Mania is a bizarre and fascinating example of a bubble: It is fascinating because in this case, the underlying asset was a common or garden tulip bulb, a flower that had recently been introduced to Holland and that was, at the time, new and exotic. At the peak of the bubble in February 1637, tulip contracts sold for more than 10 times the annual income of a skilled craftsman. My favorite story from this period is that of a rich Dutch merchant who returned home one evening to his Amsterdam townhome to find that the maid had eaten his prize tulip bulb, thinking it was an onion.[5]

THE ROARING TWENTIES

The first example of a financial bubble in the twentieth century emerged in the 1920s. At this time, most economists believed that markets function smoothly and that capitalism, if left to itself, will deliver prosperity. Although they recognized that market systems lead to regular swings in economic activity, most economists viewed fluctuations as minor and the system itself as self-correcting. This intellectual climate reflected the economic reality of the times: the roaring twenties.

Calvin Coolidge, U.S. president from 1923 to 1929, was a staunch supporter of free markets, and his laissez faire policies delivered a period of remarkable prosperity and growth that was not unlike America in the 1990s and early 2000s. The mood of optimism was infectious and the public widely believed that the stock market had nowhere to go but up. This mood was buoyed by experts such as the American economist Irving Fisher, who made a fortune from the invention of the visible card index system, which he patented in 1913. His success was short-lived and he

> subsequently lost a fortune ... when he borrowed money to exercise rights to buy additional Rand shares in the bull market of the late 1920s. . . . Fisher had staked his public reputation as an economic pundit by his persistent optimism about the economy and stock prices, even after the 1929 crash. His reputation crashed too, especially among non-economists in New Haven, where the university had to buy his house and rent it to him to save him from eviction. Until the 1950s the name Irving Fisher was without honour in his own university.[6]

Fisher's blunder is one of the most famous examples of a bad call in the history of economic forecasting. His faith in the free market was painfully and tragically tested when, between 1929 and 1933, unemployment in the United States increased from 6% to 24% of the labor force and output fell 25% below trend.

Then, as now, economists and politicians were divided as to the best course of action. Herbert Hoover followed Coolidge into the White House in 1929 when Coolidge declined to run for a further term. Hoover lasted only four years, during which he presided over the worst collapse in economic activity in U.S. economic history. This was the beginning of the Great Depression, a decade-long drop in world economic output that scarred a generation and contributed in Germany to the rise of Hitler and the beginning of World War II.

THE GREAT DEPRESSION

The Great Depression caused a change in the political sphere that persists to this day. Western democracies began to recognize a vastly increased role for the federal government in the management of economic affairs, and following the Employment Act of 1946, U.S. politicians were given a much larger role in the management of the economy than they had previously enjoyed.

Why was the increased role for government accepted by the people? A major reason is that John Maynard Keynes provided a theoretical explanation of what had gone wrong. In his 1936 book, he explained what caused the Great Depression and he provided a remedy to prevent events like it from occurring again. The main difference of Keynes's ideas from those of his predecessors was his rejection of the idea that the economy is a self-regulating system. The classical economists thought that the economy, if left to itself, would quickly return to full employment. Keynes disagreed.

The classical Norwegian economist Ragnar Frisch likened the economy to a child's rocking horse. The horse is regularly buffeted by shocks. Think of a child hitting the horse with a stick. According to Frisch, these blows are like major economic events: a war in the Middle East, a hurricane in the Midwest, an airline pilots' strike. After each shock, unemployment might rise temporarily as the economy readjusted to the blow, but it would quickly return to its equilibrium level, just as the rocking horse will come to rest if left alone. This is a good physical analogy to the classical idea of a self-correcting economic system.

FIGURE 1.1 John Maynard Keynes, 1883–1946. Keynes was the most influential economist of the twentieth century. He was an academic, a civil servant, a statesman, and a journalist. Keynes's book, *The General Theory of Employment Interest and Money* (1936), transformed the role of the state in capitalist societies and was responsible for the way we currently think of the role of government in the economy. (Time & Life Pictures/Getty Images)

Keynes had much less faith in the free market. In Keynesian economics, the economy is like a boat on the ocean with a broken rudder. Gusts of wind represent major economic events: a war in the Middle East, a hurricane in the Midwest, an airline pilots' strike. After each shock, unemployment rises or falls permanently and there is no self-correcting mechanism to return it to a unique equilibrium: Just as a sailboat will be becalmed wherever it comes to rest, the unemployment rate can end up anywhere. The classical economists saw the economy as a stable self-correcting system. Keynes did not.

STAGFLATION

Keynesian economics was widely accepted after World War II as a correct description of the way the economy works. From Keynesian theory there came a prescription for how to run policy that was followed successfully for three decades, from 1940 through 1970. In recessions, the central bank should lower the interest rate to stimulate private spending and increase aggregate demand. This is called monetary policy. In recessions, the government should spend more and pay for it through increased borrowing. This is called fiscal policy.

The legacy of Keynesian economics dictates the actions that are followed to this day to combat recessions. Many academic economists have, however, lost confidence in the theory put forward by Keynes to explain why monetary and fiscal policy are appropriate and how they work.

The loss of faith in Keynesian economics occurred as a consequence of a confluence of events in the 1970s that was unexpected because it was inconsistent with the basic tenets laid out by Keynes in *The General Theory*. In 1975, unemployment rose above 9% for the first time since the Depression and at the same time inflation rose above 13%. This coincidence of inflation and unemployment was dubbed *stagflation* by contemporary writers. Since Keynesian economics claimed that high unemployment and high inflation could not occur together, academic economists abandoned Keynesian theory. But although academic economists gave up on Keynes, economic policymakers did not give up on Keynesian policies.

Recently, politicians and commentators have rediscovered Keynes, and governments around the world have begun to spend money freely that they don't have. In the United States, the Obama administration passed legislation in the fall of 2008 to enact an $800 billion fiscal stimulus to be spread out over two and a half years. In the UK, the governor of the Bank of England, Mervyn King, attacked the chancellor of the exchequer, Alistair Darling, for running "extraordinary deficits" that were predicted to cause government debt to reach 80% of GDP by 2014. The French president, Nicolas Sarkozy, engaged in a remarkable public spat with the German chancellor, Angela Merkel. In June 2009, Germany passed a balanced budget law that threatened to reduce public debt to zero, while Sarkozy went on record as favoring large government deficits as long as the economy was in trouble. These divergent policies cannot be good for the future of the euro!

The remarkable new move toward fiscal profligacy has led to discomfort among some academic economists who believe that the stagflation of the 1970s discredited the Keynesian theory that supports deficit spending as a way out of a depression. Important critics of fiscal deficits include Robert Barro of Harvard University and John Taylor of Stanford University.[7] Barro and Taylor are classical economists who believe that government intervention often does more harm than good.

Other academic economists do not have fully worked-out theories of the crisis but are willing to back the fiscal stimulus because they believe that Keynesian economics is sound and that there is no good alternative to save the global economy. Writing in the *New York Times*, Paul Krugman dismisses arguments by John Taylor and Eugene Fama against the stimulus on the grounds that their arguments are without substance and are politically motivated. Krugman is persuaded by Keynesian ideas but is still searching for a sound economic model with which to expound them:

> I'm on a continuing quest to develop a tractable model. . . . Why? you may ask. Why not go with verbal intuition? Well, I'm enough of a conventional economist to think that there's no substitute for a model with dotted i's and crossed t's; it's not *the truth*, but it really does help clarify your thinking. (Krugman, 2009; emphasis in original)

Krugman is right. In order to move the debate forward, it is essential that economists have a common framework to understand what went wrong and how to correct it. U.S. critics of the Obama fiscal spending plan such as Barro, Fama, and Taylor are not just opposed to the plan on purely political grounds, although that surely contributes to their opposition to the proposed increase in the size of government. More fundamentally, Keynesian economists in the Obama administration and their supporters in academia and in the media have not provided an internally consistent theory that explains why the free market fails to deliver full employment.

Keynes's book, *The General Theory,* did not provide such a theory. The book is difficult to read, internally incoherent, and inconsistent with a body of economic theory that has been widely accepted for at least 200 years. More important, it is inconsistent with the existence of the stagflation that we observed in the 1970s. According to Keynes, we should expect to see high inflation or high unemployment, but not both at once. In the absence of a consistent theory that explains why free markets sometimes fail, conservative critics of the Obama fiscal stimulus retreated into a body of classical ideas that provides a different answer to the crisis. According to them, government is the problem and not the solution.

WHY FISCAL POLICY IS THE WRONG APPROACH

This book explains the progression of thought from classical to Keynesian ideas. But it is much more than that. I also have something new to say that is neither Keynesian nor classical. Economists use models of the economy to nail down their assumptions about how the economy works. A model is a mathematical description of an economic theory, and a good model is synonymous with a good theory. Krugman is right in his assertion that there is no substitute for "a model with dotted i's and crossed t's" since it is by modeling the economy that we make our ideas precise.

When I began the project that I describe in this book, I intended to find such a model. I believed that it would provide the missing intellectual foundation to Keynesian economics. I wanted to fix *The General Theory* by showing how Keynes could be made consistent with the rest of economics. I thought that this fix would enable me to understand stagflation and I expected that my work would explain why the Obama fiscal stimulus is the right way to restore full employment.

But the deeper I got into the project, the more I realized that to fix Keynesian economics, I also had to change it. Keynes's fundamental proposition is that the free market is not self-stabilizing. I agree with that proposition and I share my belief with Keynesians such as Paul Krugman. But in providing a formal explanation of why Keynes was right, I grew to believe that fiscal policy may not be the best remedy. Although the fundamental ideas of *The General Theory* are correct, the details of the theory that led Keynesians to propose additional government expenditure are wrong.

Keynes advocated fiscal policy because he thought that private firms were not investing enough during the Great Depression. He thought that consumption would go up automatically when income went up because people spend a fixed fraction of their income and save the rest. But two decades of research in the 1950s and 1960s showed that consumption does not depend on income: It depends on wealth. When government spends more, households save more. They know that the government will not be able to provide for their retirements in the future if it has a huge debt to repay. That is exactly what happened in the United States, the UK, and Europe in 2009 in response to the fiscal stimulus; the increase in saving partially offset the positive effect of the increased expenditure by government. Fiscal policy *can* help the economy out of the recession; but it is not nearly as effective as the Keynesians think, and the cost will be a permanent increase in the size of the government sector that will be paid for by our grandchildren.

The director of the National Economic Council in the Obama administration is Larry Summers, former president of Harvard, former secretary of the Treasury, former chief economist at the World Bank, and an academic economist of considerable standing in the profession. Summers is a nephew of two eminent Nobel Laureates in economics, Ken Arrow of Stanford University and Paul Samuelson of MIT. Arrow is known for his work on general equilibrium theory, a body of ideas that lies at the heart of classical economics. Samuelson, who died in December of 2009, was one of the world's most distinguished living Keynesians.

He is responsible for the way that almost all academics and policymakers interpret Keynes today.

My main theme in this book is that the way that Samuelson proposed to reconcile Keynes with general equilibrium theory is wrong. When Samuelson's theory is combined with modern explanations of how people form their expectations of the future, it misses the main message of Keynes: High unemployment can persist forever.

WHAT GOVERNMENTS SHOULD DO INSTEAD

Although I believe that Keynes had a lot of important things to say, I am not a Keynesian. Instead, I will describe a new theory of macroeconomics that goes beyond classical and Keynesian theories. I will combine the main ideas from Keynesian economics with classical thought. A central part of my new theory is that the beliefs of market participants in the value of the stock market matter, and they can have an *independent* influence on economic activity. Confidence matters: A loss of confidence can become a self-fulfilling prophecy and lead to a downward spiral in economic activity that ends in a depression.[8]

Monetary and fiscal policy *may* have the effect their proponents claim, but only if households and firms regain confidence in the economy by buying tangible assets such as houses and by putting their wealth into the stock market so that firms will start to invest again in factories, and machines. There is no sound economic reason that this will occur just because government borrows money and spends it on goods and services.

If households maintain the pessimistic belief that houses, factories, and machines are worth less than they were before the recession began, this belief will be self-fulfilling.

Confidence matters. It is a separate, *independent* factor that helps to determine the unemployment rate. If we do not restore confidence, the economy may begin to grow again, but the private sector will not create the jobs that are required to restore full employment.

Just as confidence can be too low, it can also be too high. If confidence builds too quickly, bubbles will arise in the asset markets that can lead the economy to have *too much* employment. When the economy grows too fast, it is harder for the central bank to control inflation. Bubbles and crashes are both harmful to economic well-being. To counteract the effect of swings in confidence, I propose a new policy that does not involve large fiscal deficits and that is a simple extension of the current central bank policy of interest rate control. I will argue that central banks throughout the world should intervene in markets to prevent wild swings in stock market prices, and I will explain why this makes sense.

A NEW PARADIGM AND A NEW POLICY

Some economists have suggested that central banks should raise domestic interest rates to prick stock market bubbles and lower them to prevent market crashes. This is not what I am advocating. Rather, I propose that the Bank of England, the Federal Reserve, and the European Central Bank should engage in a concerted effort with other national central banks to target domestic stock market indices in addition to their traditional role of setting domestic interest rates. My proposal allows a nation's central bank to use variations in the domestic interest rate to fight inflation and variations in the growth rate of a national stock price index to manage confidence and select a high employment equilibrium.

My policy proposal is based on a new theory that combines the best features of classical and Keynesian economics.

From classical economics, I take the idea that a sound theory must explain how individuals behave and how their collective choices determine aggregate outcomes. From Keynesian economics, I take the idea that markets do not always work well and that sometimes capitalism needs some guidance. These ideas form a coherent new paradigm for macroeconomics in the twenty-first century. It is my hope that we can design ways of correcting the excesses of free market economies that preserve the best features of capitalism without stifling entrepreneurship and without adopting the inefficiencies of centrally planned economies. The following pages show how.

CHAPTER 2

Classical Economics

It is not from the benevolence of the butcher, the brewer, or the baker that
we expect our dinner, but from their regard to their own interest.

—Adam Smith (1776)

This quote from Adam Smith, the father of modern economics, summarizes the most important idea of classical economics. Selfish behavior by individuals leads to an outcome that benefits everyone in society. Smith wrote his most important book, *An Inquiry into the Nature and Causes of the Wealth of Nations*, in 1776, the same year the Declaration of Independence was adopted in Philadelphia. After the publication of the *Wealth of Nations*, economists refined the ideas it contained and developed them into a body of classical economic theory. What is classical economics and why should it interest you?

Classical economics can be split into two parts: *general equilibrium theory* and the *quantity theory of money*. General equilibrium theory was developed in 1874 by a French economist, Léon Walras, who taught at the University of Lausanne in Switzerland.[1] It explains how much of every good is produced and how the price of each good is set relative to every other good. For example, general equilibrium theory aims to tell us what determines how many hours will be worked by every person in the world, the number

FIGURE 2.1 Adam Smith, 1723–1790. Smith, the Scottish philosopher and economist, is widely credited as the father of modern economics. His book *An Inquiry into the Nature and Causes of the Wealth of Nations,* first published in 1776, was the first modern book in economics. Smith was a product of the Scottish Enlightenment, a renaissance of thought that swept eighteenth-century Scotland. (Time & Life Pictures/Getty Images)

of cars produced in Japan, and the number of hours you would need to work to be able to afford a golfing holiday in Scotland.

The quantity theory of money was developed by David Hume, a Scottish philosopher and economist who was a leading figure in the Scottish Enlightenment and a contemporary of Adam Smith. The Scottish Enlightenment

FIGURE 2.2 David Hume, 1711–1776. Hume was a Scottish philosopher, economist, and historian who, along with Adam Smith, was one of the most important figures in the Scottish Enlightenment. He was one of the earliest economists to recognize a connection between money and inflation, which he described in the essay "Of Money." (Getty Images)

was a period of remarkable intellectual achievement in eighteenth-century Scotland that produced the economists Adam Smith and James Mill, the architect Robert Adam, the inventor of the steam engine James Watt, and the novelist and poet Sir Walter Scott.[2]

Quantity theory is about money prices as opposed to real quantities and relative prices. It aims to tell us what determines how many dollars, pounds, or yen the average person will earn for an hour's work, or the dollar, pound, or yen price you will have to pay for a car and the money cost of your hotel bill when you arrive in St. Andrews and tee up for the first hole. The quantity theory of money is also used to understand what determines the rate of inflation.

Classical economics, as embodied in general equilibrium theory and the quantity theory of money, is worth understanding because it has influenced the thinking of all living economists. This includes academics, journalists, and policy economists in business, central banks, or government. Even those who reject its relevance as an explanation of the real world still use classical economics as a benchmark against which to measure the performance of real-world economies. How can we tell if one mode of economic organization is better than another? What does it mean for an organization to waste resources? These concepts are given meaning within classical theory, and classical economists have shown that, under some circumstances, distributing commodities using markets is the best that a society can hope to do.

HOW THE ECONOMIC PIECES FIT TOGETHER

General equilibrium theory, developed by Walras, is a beautiful and elegant description of how the whole economy fits together. Contemporary British economists had worked out the theory of demand and supply one market at a time. Walras put all the markets together and showed how prices are determined and how they coordinate the actions of hundreds of millions of unrelated individuals.

FIGURE 2.3 Alfred Marshall, 1842–1924. Marshall was one of the leading economists of the nineteenth century. He taught at Cambridge, England, where he developed the model of demand and supply that explains how quantity and price are determined in a single market. His book, *Principles of Economics* (1920, 8th edition), influenced the teaching of economics for 50 years. (University of Bristol)

Human beings make plans and try to realize them. But they don't do it in a vacuum. Every decision that you and I make is constrained in some way. Constraints may be codified into laws—or they may simply be a result of implicit social conventions. The fundamental problem of the social sciences is to explain how free-thinking human beings act subject to constraints that are themselves determined by the actions of those same individuals. General equilibrium theory is a solution to a special case of this problem: the interactions of individuals in markets.

General equilibrium theory is built on the theory of demand and supply that was described in its modern form by Alfred Marshall in his book *Principles of Economics*.[3] Marshall taught economics at St. Johns College Cambridge in the 1860s having "moved from mathematics to economics via ethics which he abandoned as a waste of time."[4] He was born into a clerical family and his father, a cashier at the Bank of England, planned for the young Alfred to become a priest.

During the late nineteenth century, Cambridge philosophers were in the process of replacing religion with an alternative secular, ethical, and moral system. Under the influence of Cambridge philosophy, Marshall declared himself an agnostic, and rather than enter the church, he devoted his life to the establishment of English economics. He was the teacher not only of John Maynard Keynes but also of Neville Keynes, John Maynard's father.[5]

Marshall's theory of demand and supply explained how much of any given commodity is produced and the price at which it is bought and sold. Walras applied the theory of demand and supply to all of the commodities in the economy at the same time. He asked the question: Is there a system of prices, one for every good, such that the quantities demanded and supplied of every commodity are equal simultaneously? Since Walras first posed the question, it has been extensively studied, and we now know that the answer is yes.

Although that may not sound like much, it's a considerable intellectual achievement. To answer Walras's question, you need to account for all of the possible connections among markets. If the price of oil goes up, that will affect the demand for public transport and it will increase the number of taxis needed in London. Will there be enough workers to

FIGURE 2.4 Léon Walras, 1834–1910. Walras was a French-born economist who taught at the University of Lausanne in Switzerland. Along with Stanley Jevons and Carl Menger, he created the marginal revolution in economics, the idea that it is the last person hired that determines how much all workers will be paid. Walras took this idea further than Jevons or Menger by developing general equilibrium theory. (UNIL/Archives)

produce the extra taxis? At what wage? Under quite general conditions, economists have shown that there is at least one system of quantities and prices, including wages and labor allocated to each industry, under which the demands and supplies of all commodities are in balance all at once. Walras showed that capitalism can work in theory. But does it work in practice?

DO MARKETS WORK WELL?

Walras's successor at the University of Lausanne was Vilfredo Pareto. Pareto was not just concerned with the existence of an economic equilibrium. He wanted to know if free markets allocate resources among different members of society in the best possible way. Pareto is the father of modern welfare economics, an inquiry into the properties of different ways of distributing goods and their impact on human well-being.

Pareto was born in Paris in 1848 to Italian exiles. He later moved to Italy to complete his education in Turin, where he studied mathematics and literature. After graduating from the Polytechnic Institute, he worked as a railroad engineer and only in his early forties did Pareto turn to economics. But even though he did not formally study economics until later in life, Pareto was an active critic of the Italian government's economic policies for many years, and early in life he published a number of pamphlets denouncing protectionist economic policies and opposing militarism.[6]

Pareto is known to economists for asking the question: Could an omniscient planner reallocate commodities among all the different people in the world in a better way than the free market? Under Pareto's definition of "better," the answer was a resounding no. In other words, markets do just about as good a job of allocating resources as anyone could possibly imagine.

The planner is a fictitious character who symbolizes perfect knowledge. An omniscient planner would need to know everything about the preferences of every person

FIGURE 2.5 Vilfredo Pareto, 1848–1923. Pareto was an Italian sociologist, economist, and philosopher. Born in France of an exiled noble Genoese family, he succeeded Walras at the University of Lausanne as a lecturer in economics and is best known for the concept of Pareto efficiency. Pareto also worked on the income distribution, and the Pareto distribution in statistics is named after him. (The Granger Collection, New York)

in the world, and he would need full knowledge about the technology for producing every commodity. Since this level of knowledge is impossible for any single individual to acquire, the implication of Pareto's work is that markets work far better than socialist planning of the kind that was tried in the Soviet Union in the twentieth century. The planner symbolizes perfect knowledge, and he does not exist in practice. The free market is a practical mechanism that accumulates information and transmits it from one person to another in a way that approximates this unattainable ideal.

Although Pareto's work implies that free markets work well, this proposition rests on a set of assumptions about the properties of technology and the way people behave. By laying out these assumptions, Pareto provided the groundwork for later economists to ask a related question: Under what circumstances does the free market break down? That is the question we are all facing today.

Pareto's concept of a better allocation of commodities is so important that it has been formalized in economics in the form of a theorem called the first theorem of welfare economics. The *first welfare theorem* says that there is a connection between Pareto's notion of a better allocation of commodities and the way that commodities are allocated in market economies. Pareto's notion of a better allocation says nothing about who is rich and who is poor; he takes this as given. It simply says that markets allocate resources efficiently given the existing distribution of wealth. Economists call the notion of a better allocation, embodied in Pareto's work, *Pareto efficiency*. The first welfare theorem is the statement that every competitive equilibrium is Pareto efficient.

The notion that markets are Pareto efficient is behind the reverence that economists have for free markets. It captures the idea of the invisible hand that Adam Smith wrote about in 1776. In Smith's words,

> By preferring the support of domestic to that of foreign industry, [every individual] intends only his own security; and by directing

that industry in such a manner as its produce may be of the greatest value, he intends only his own gain, and he is in this, as in many other cases, *led by an invisible hand to promote an end which was no part of his intention.* Nor is it always the worse for the society that it was no part of it. By pursuing his own interest he frequently promotes that of the society more effectually than when he really intends to promote it. I have never known much good done by those who affected to trade for the public good. (Smith, 1776, chapter 2, book 4, p. 477; emphasis added)

There are some important ideas in this quote that still resonate today. First, selfishness promotes the public good because the profit motive leads firms to produce commodities that people want to buy. This idea is at the root of the modern conservative's defense of private enterprise. Second, beware of people who claim to be acting in your interests. This second idea is at the root of the distrust that many critics have of government regulation of markets.

The first welfare theorem is important because one of the commodities allocated by markets is the time that each person spends in paid employment. If markets worked in the way that general equilibrium theory asserts they do, all unemployment would be the voluntary choice of individuals to spend more time looking for a higher paying job. This seems like a tough sell as a description of the world economy of 2008–2009, where auto workers in Detroit, oil refinery workers in England, and construction workers in France were laid off in the thousands. In the United States alone, half a million workers lost their jobs every month in the first few months of 2009. Because these people were not voluntarily choosing a prolonged vacation, we are forced to the conclusion that the first welfare theorem does not apply to real economies.

Because the conclusions of the theorem follow logically from its assumptions, one of the conditions for the first welfare theorem to hold must be violated. But which one? I will return to this question in chapter 7, where I will explain that the welfare theorem requires market participants to have more information than is reasonable: Because some people have private information, some markets may fail to exist.

A MARK, A YEN, A BUCK, OR A POUND...

General equilibrium is a powerful tool that explains why people trade with each other, and how much of each product people and firms produce. It does not explain why people use money or how the dollar values of prices are set. Classical economics explains these features of modern economies with the quantity theory of money.

Money has been used to buy and sell commodities for as long as human beings have lived in organized societies. Precious metals were used as a means of exchange by the Babylonians in 3000 BC. In China, cowrie shells were used as money beginning in the twelfth century BC. By 500 BC, the Chinese were using coins made of precious metals and India developed them at about the same time. The evolution from a commodity money such as the cowrie shell through the use of precious metals and eventually to a paper money is typical in the history of world civilizations, although the speed of transition varies enormously across continents and cultures.

Historically, money has often consisted of one or more precious metals. Gold was used for international transactions in medieval Europe, whereas silver and copper coins were used domestically.[7] When Europeans discovered America, there was an influx of gold into Europe from mines in the New World, and contemporary observers noticed that this was accompanied by an increase in the general level of prices.

One of the earliest writers on the subject of money was the English philosopher David Hume, who wrote a delightful and insightful essay, *Of Money*, which is as relevant today as it was when he wrote it in 1752.[8]

David Hume and his contemporaries developed the *quantity theory of money*, which asserts that the money value of all of the goods and services produced in a given year (the money value of gross domestic product, or GDP) is proportional to the stock of money. The classical economists used general equilibrium theory to determine the physical quantities of goods and services that would be produced and to determine their prices relative to each other. These are called *relative prices*. They used the quantity theory of money to determine the average level of prices in terms of money. These are called *money prices* or nominal prices.

. . . IS ALL THAT MAKES THE WORLD GO AROUND

The difference between relative prices, determined by general equilibrium theory, and money prices, determined by the quantity theory of money, is this. Suppose that Denis, the last worker hired by the Aluminum Box Company, can produce 40 boxes per week by working for 40 hours.[9] Classical general equilibrium theory predicts that the wage paid to Denis would be one commodity per hour. It has nothing to say about the money wage or the money price of an aluminum box. These money prices remain unexplained by the theory. In equilibrium, it might be that Denis earns $1 an hour and an aluminum box costs

$1, or Denis earns $10 an hour and an aluminum box costs $10. Both situations are equally consistent with the theory of relative prices contained in general equilibrium theory.

That's where the quantity theory of money comes in. According to the quantity theory, the dollar price of a commodity depends on how many dollars are circulating since dollars are needed to facilitate exchange. In Hume's words,

> Money is not, properly speaking, one of the subjects of commerce; but only the instrument which men have agreed upon to facilitate the exchange of one commodity for another. It is none of the wheels of trade: It is the oil which renders the motion of the wheels more smooth and easy. (Hume, 1754, p. 281)

The idea that money is the oil that keeps the wheels turning is very powerful, and some version of it is built into every modern interpretation of classical economics. At its core is the notion that real economic activity is determined by the fundamentals of the economy—preferences, endowments, and technology—and that, in the long run, the quantity of money determines only the price level. This idea is expressed by the proposition that, in the long run, *money is neutral*.

HELICOPTER BEN

People often misunderstand the *neutrality of money*, and it is sometimes asserted that the quantity theory predicts that a doubling of the quantity of money will lead to a doubling of the price level but will have no effect on real economic activity. The chairman of the Fed, Ben Bernanke, is sometimes referred to irreverently as "Helicopter Ben" because, in a speech, he referred to the following example from the writing of the economist and Nobel Laureate Milton Friedman (1994, p. 29).

Friedman asked us to consider what would happen if a helicopter were to fly over a country and drop dollar bills. A crude rendition of the quantity theory would assert that the effect would be an immediate doubling of all money prices and all quantities traded would remain unchanged. Everybody would wake up on Wednesday morning, after a helicopter drop on Tuesday night, and a cup of coffee that cost $1 on Tuesday would cost $2 on Wednesday. But the theory is much more sophisticated than that. Although it asserts that money has no long-run effect on employment or output, the quantity theorists do not make that assertion about the short run because the evidence suggests otherwise. In practice, it takes time for the effect of an increase in the stock of money to work its way through the economy.

There is a tension between general equilibrium theory and the quantity theory of money that persists in economics to this day. General equilibrium theory predicts that relative prices will be determined to equate the quantities demanded and supplied for all commodities simultaneously. The quantity theory of money predicts that the general level of prices will be proportional to the stock of money. But when new money enters the economy, all prices do not change overnight. Hence, during the transition from the short run to the long run, the predictions of the general equilibrium model and the long-run predictions of the quantity theory cannot both be true. Economists attribute the difference between the two theories to the effects of economic frictions.

ECONOMIC FRICTIONS

Economists view general equilibrium theory as an idealized description of the way a set of interrelated markets might work: But at any point in time, there are frictions that prevent the exact equality of demand and supply.

Economists use the word "friction" to mean a restriction on trade or a cost of changing a price that prevents firms from adjusting wages and prices quickly to the levels that are predicted by general equilibrium theory. The analogy is to the laws of physics, where friction interferes with Newton's laws of motion. These laws do not hold exactly in experimental situations because of the difficulty of setting up ideal conditions. Physicists take account of friction to explain the motion of an object down an inclined plane or the energy loss in a motor. Economists invoke economic friction to explain why all prices do not change overnight in response to an increase in the quantity of money.

When the model of demand and supply is applied to the labor market, it implies that the quantity of labor demanded should be equal to the quantity of labor supplied. Because we often observe high unemployment, economists argue that this unemployment must be due to an economic friction that slows down the adjustment of the wage. Large frictions imply that prices and wages adjust slowly and so there is a higher chance of seeing high and persistent unemployment.

In the 1930s, the United States experienced a period of unemployment in excess of 15% for six years in a row. It was difficult to reconcile this with classical theory and, as a result, Keynes developed a new approach in which he threw out the model of demand and supply in the labor market. For roughly 30 years, his alternative theory of how the economy works dominated the profession. It contained an explanation of what happened in the Depression and how to correct it, and it led to a fundamental change in political systems that persists to this day.

CHAPTER 3

The Impact of Keynes on the World Economy

> *For my part I think that capitalism, wisely managed, can probably be made more efficient for attaining economic ends than any alternative system yet in sight, but that in itself it is in many ways extremely objectionable.*
>
> —John Maynard Keynes (1931, p. 321)

The influence of Keynes on economics and politics was profound. Before Keynesian economics, the role of the state in economic affairs was limited to a few areas such as the provision of defense and the maintenance of the legal system. After Keynes wrote *The General Theory*, Western governments took on the added role of maintaining a high and stable level of employment. To understand the debate between classical economists such as Eugene Fama and Keynesian economists such as Paul Krugman, we must come to grips with how and why this transition occurred.

Keynes's new vision of the economy was itself a journey of escape from old ways of thinking. He was trained in classical economics and was well aware of its strengths as well as its weaknesses. But the Great Depression had a profound influence on all economists in much the same way that the 2008 financial crisis is influencing economists today. Keynes realized that Adam Smith's vision of the invisible hand needed to be amended to allow for the immense human misery that occurred during this period. Long and protracted periods of unemployment were not consistent with classical ideas. It was time for something new.

MAYNARD KEYNES'S NEW VISION

Keynesian economics was different from everything that went before. In the 1920s, the classical economists saw the economy as a stable self-correcting machine. Random unpredictable events might cause a disturbance to the economy that would temporarily throw some people out of work. But hundreds of millions of selfish individuals would be guided, in the words of Adam Smith, "by an invisible hand," to move the economy quickly back to full employment.

Keynes was much more skeptical of the self-correcting nature of the economy because he saw no evidence of it in Great Britain during the 1920s, when unemployment remained high for a decade. In his view, one of the most important shocks to the economy is a shock to the confidence of investors about the future value of the stock market. He called this the "animal spirits of investors." When combined with Keynes's theory of the labor market, the possibility that markets may be driven by confidence implied that very high unemployment could persist for a very long time for no good reason.

The classical economists believed that excessive unemployment could only occur in the short run, a temporary period needed for prices to adjust to their long-run equilibrium levels. When writing about his view of the long run and the short run in 1924, Keynes famously asserted that. "In the long run we are all dead!"[1]

UNEMPLOYMENT DURING THE GREAT DEPRESSION

Business cycles are not new. The United States underwent five major financial crises in the nineteenth century, and all of them had some elements in common. British economist Arthur Pigou summarized contemporary views of the theory of business cycles in an influential book, *Industrial Fluctuations*, published in 1929.[2] He listed at least six different causes of business cycles including errors of optimism and pessimism, agricultural fluctuations caused by the weather, shocks to productivity as a consequence of new inventions, monetary fluctuations, industrial disputes, and changes in tastes. Nobody at this time disputed the fact that, left to itself, the economy would quickly return to full employment after one of these six factors caused a disturbance. The Great Depression of the 1930s changed this view forever.

Figure 3.2 plots the percentage of unemployed persons in the United States from 1890 through 2007. The ups and downs that occur at irregular intervals are a manifestation of business cycles, and it is these ups and downs that Pigou attributed to a laundry list of possible causes, from optimism and pessimism to changes in tastes.

There are two features of the graph worth noting. First, the upward spike that began in 1929 and ended in 1941 is much larger than any spike in unemployment that has occurred before or since. The closest episode is the recession that occurred in the last decade of the nineteenth century, in which unemployment reached 18% and exceeded 10% for six years in a row. Second, fluctuations in the unemployment

FIGURE 3.1 Arthur C. Pigou, 1887–1959. The British economist Arthur C. Pigou was a student of Alfred Marshall and a professor at Cambridge. He is best known for his book *The Economics of Welfare* (1933). He also wrote *Industrial Fluctuations* (1929), which was about the causes of business cycles. (The Department of Economics, Louisiana State University)

rate since 1946 have been less volatile than fluctuations before World War II.

Keynesian economists claim, and I think they are right, that the reduction in the size of fluctuations in the United States after World War II is a direct consequence of the increase in the role of government that followed when Congress passed a new piece of legislation, the Employment Act of 1946, that encouraged the government to "promote maximum employment, production, and purchasing

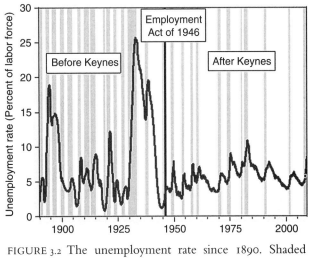

FIGURE 3.2 The unemployment rate since 1890. Shaded areas are NBER recessions.

power." The increased stability of postwar business cycles in the United States is direct evidence for the success of Keynesian economics.

KEYNES'S ESCAPE FROM CLASSICAL ECONOMICS

In the 1920s, Keynes was a classical economist. The Great Depression caused him to change his views and to develop an alternative theory that would justify policies that he believed were the right way to cure what he saw as a massive social ill. It was one thing to be sure of oneself and another to explain why state-of-the-art economic theory was wrong. As Keynes put it in the opening chapter of *The General Theory*,

> The classical theorists resemble Euclidian geometers in a non-Euclidian world who, discovering that straight lines apparently

parallel often meet, rebuke the lines for not keeping straight—as the only remedy for the unfortunate collisions which are occurring. Yet, in truth, there is no remedy except to throw over the axiom of parallels and to work out a non-Euclidian geometry.

This revolutionary idea would overturn existing economic thought and put a major dent in the notion of the unregulated capitalist economy as a self-correcting system.

Classical ideas at the time were summarized by the theory laid out by Pigou in *Industrial Fluctuations*. According to these ideas, the Depression must have been caused by one of the six fundamental factors listed previously: These included errors of optimism and pessimism, agricultural fluctuations caused by the weather, shocks to productivity as a consequence of new inventions, monetary fluctuations, industrial disputes, or changes in tastes. Some modern business cycle theorists go further. They would claim that all shocks are caused by fundamental changes and most of these are due to the introduction of new technology: But whatever the origin of the shock, classical theory implies that the economy should quickly return to full employment.

There are two major problems with this position. First, it is difficult to identify a fundamental shock of significant importance that could have triggered a depression of the magnitude that was experienced in the 1930s. Second, whatever this shock might have been, the millions of workers who lost their jobs in the early years should have quickly found new employment. The reality was very different and the cost in terms of human misery was incalculable.

KEYNESIAN THEORY

As an alternative to the classical model of demand and supply, Keynes threw away the labor supply curve, one of the equations that economists used to describe a rest point of the classical economic system. He replaced this equation with the assumption that the confidence of investors is an independent driving force of business cycles. In one stroke, this solved both problems of the classical system. According to Keynes, the impulse that caused the Great Depression was a spontaneous fall in confidence about the future—a kind of mass hysteria affecting all stock market participants simultaneously. It was the stock market crash that *caused* the Great Depression.

How did this work? The stock market fell because people believed that the machines and factories that produce profit would, in the future, have a much lower value. Firms stopped buying new capital equipment and the workers who produced capital goods became unemployed. These workers stopped buying consumer goods and workers who produced these goods also lost their jobs.

The economy did not return to full employment because there is no self-correcting mechanism of the kind envisaged by Pigou and his contemporaries. In Keynes's view, any unemployment rate can persist forever because the forces that tend to restore equilibrium are either nonexistent or so weak that we would not expect to see them operating in finite time.

Keynes's theory of what went wrong in the Great Depression is based on the twin concepts of aggregate demand and aggregate supply. Aggregate demand and supply are similar to, but distinct from, Marshall's theory of demand and supply in a single market. It is important not to confuse the two concepts. Aggregate demand explains the total money value of goods and services that all households and firms would like to spend in a given period of time. Aggregate supply explains how many workers are needed to produce the goods and services necessary to meet that demand.

KEYNESIAN POLICY

Before Keynes, most people believed that government should "live within its means." This position is exemplified by a 1932 speech that Herbert Hoover gave at Madison Square Garden in his failed reelection bid.

> The Federal Government has been forced in this emergency to unusual expenditure, but in partial alleviation of these extraordinary and unusual expenditures *the Republican administration has made a successful effort to reduce the ordinary running expenses of the Government.* (Hoover, 1932; emphasis added)

In contrast to this classical view that government should try to balance its budget in a recession, Keynes argued instead that the government should borrow money and use it to stimulate aggregate demand. He explained why this was appropriate with his new economic theory.

In classical economics, every dollar spent by government is one less dollar spent by households because the size of the pie is fixed. In Keynesian economics, an extra dollar spent by government increases the size of the pie and causes an increase in the amount available to both government and households. Keynes argued that, to escape from a depression, national governments should borrow and use the borrowed money to purchase goods and services from private firms. This theory of why governments should run fiscal deficits was used by President Nicolas Sarkozy in France, Chancellor of the Exchequer Alistair Darling in the UK, and Treasury Secretary Timothy Geithner in the United States to justify huge increases in public sector borrowing in these countries in 2008–2009.

Franklin Delano Roosevelt initiated modest public works programs in the 1930s, in an attempt to pull the

U.S. economy out of the Great Depression. But they were too small to have much effect, and the federal deficits of the 1930s were offset to a large extent by contractions in state budgets, much as happened in the United States in 2009.[3] Deficit spending on a large scale started in earnest when the United States entered World War II, and at this time, Keynesian policies were dramatically successful.

The massive fiscal expansion in the early years of World War II coincided with the emergence of the U.S. economy from the Great Depression. The economy rebounded from the slump and in the early 1940s, unemployment fell to historically low levels, GDP growth accelerated, and output per person finally caught up with where it would have been if the Depression had not occurred. This is the result that Keynes had predicted. He argued that if private investment expenditure is too low, it must be replaced by government investment expenditure. The success of the Keynesian explanation of these events led the Nobel Prize–winning economist Milton Friedman to assert in a 1965 interview with *Time* magazine that "We Are All Keynesians Now."[4]

Where the Keynesians Lost Their Way

> *The basic Keynesian analysis of this question [fiscal stimulus] is simply wrong. Professional economists abandoned it 30 years ago when Bob Lucas, Tom Sargent and Ed Prescott pointed out its logical inconsistencies. It has not appeared in graduate programmes or professional journals since.*
>
> —John Cochrane (March 18, 2009, writing in an online debate for *The Economist* magazine)

Clearly, not every economist is a Keynesian. John Cochrane, who penned these words, is a leading economist at the University of Chicago and the author of an influential graduate textbook on the theory of finance.[1] The economists he calls upon to support his argument include two Nobel Laureates, Robert Lucas and Edward Prescott, and Tom Sargent, one of the most creative and influential macroeconomists alive today. But is Cochrane right? And what are these logical inconsistencies that led him to be so skeptical of Keynesian ideas?

I studied economics as an undergraduate in England. When I graduated in the late 1970s, Keynesian economics was still widely taught to undergraduate and graduate students as *the* theory of business cycles. By the time

I completed my Ph.D. in Canada, in the early 1980s, Keynesian economics was quickly disappearing from the curricula at major universities in the UK, Canada, and the United States. The world had changed and economic thinking reflected this fact. The loss of faith in Keynesian ideas led to a resurgence of classical economics and a considerable increase in the mathematical techniques required to understand macroeconomics. With the demise of Keynesian economics came the birth of a new theoretical approach.

Keynesian economics was discredited by the rise and fall an idea: the Phillips curve. It was introduced to economics in 1958 by a New Zealander, Alban W. Phillips, known as Bill Phillips to his friends and family. Bill Phillips was an engineer by training. His enduring contribution to the literature of economics was to point out that there had been an inverse relationship between unemployment and the rate of change of money wages in a century of UK data. Historically, when unemployment had been low, wages would rise. When it had been high, they would fall.[2]

Keynesian economists embraced the Phillips curve, which they saw as empirical evidence in support of Keynesian economics. They argued that the government must choose high inflation or low unemployment by picking a point on the Phillips curve. But when the theory was put to the test, the predictions of the Keynesians failed dramatically. In place of the Phillips curve, economists introduced a new idea. The economy gravitates toward a natural rate of unemployment that cannot be influenced by fiscal or monetary policy. This chapter is about how this theory, called *the natural rate hypothesis*, came to dominate the thinking of all modern economists.

KEYNES'S THEORY OF PRICES

Although Keynesian fiscal policies were successful in restoring full employment in World War II, postwar experiments with deficit spending were less successful. During the 1960s, the United States became embroiled in an unpopular conflict in Vietnam that was difficult to finance by raising taxes. The government resorted instead to ever larger increases in government borrowing to pay for military expenditures.

Keynesian theory predicted that these deficits should have led first to full employment, and only then to inflation. Instead, the policy proved to be inflationary without leading to a reduction in the unemployment rate. In 1975, the unemployment rate reached 9% and inflation peaked at 13%. The press dubbed this new condition "stagflation." The coincidence of high inflation and high unemployment caused a crisis in economic thinking because stagflation was inconsistent with Keynesian economic thought.

According to the Keynesian theory of aggregate demand, when the Fed lowers the interest rate, demand will increase because investors are more willing to build additional machines and factories. If the government raises the tax rate, aggregate demand will decrease because households and businesses have less money to spend on goods of all kinds. When Mervyn King, Ben Bernanke, or Larry Summers talks about "managing aggregate demand," they are referring to this theory.

To understand how changes in aggregate demand are transmitted to changes in employment, Keynes added a theory of aggregate supply. The theory of aggregate supply is much more controversial, because it implies that unemployment and inflation don't occur together. This theory came back to haunt the postwar Keynesians because the prediction was directly contradicted by postwar facts. Let's see what happened when the theory was put to the test.

BILL PHILLIPS AND HIS MACHINE

Bill Phillips studied a century of data on the relationship between wage inflation and unemployment in the United Kingdom.

Phillips was an engineer by training and he is known not only for his work on inflation but also for the construction of a working analog hydraulic computer that used colored water flowing around pipes to explain Keynesian economics. Phillips demonstrated his hydraulic computer at a 1949 London School of Economics seminar, during which he gave an exposition of Keynesian economics, illustrated by a simulation of key features of Keynesian theory using his device. Figure 4.1 shows Phillips with a prototype of the machine, one of which is now in the Science Museum in London.[3] According to Chris Bissell, writing in an engineering journal, ". . . users [and observers of the machine] were enthusiastic about the way the device gave a 'feel' for economic behavior, presented visual (rather than numerical) results, and was accessible without explicit advanced mathematics."

BILL PHILLIPS AND HIS CURVE

But Bill Phillips is best known for his work on inflation. He found that in the UK data, money wages fell when unemployment was high and they rose when it was low. He graphed this relationship between unemployment and wage inflation on a diagram that now bears his name—the Phillips curve. His work was important,

FIGURE 4.1 Alban W. ("Bill") Phillips, 1914–1975. Bill
Phillips was a New Zealand–born economist who taught
at the London School of Economics (LSE) and is known
for the "Phillips curve." As a student at LSE, he developed a
machine to mimic the UK economy in which water flowed
around pipes. One of the Phillips machines is now in the
Science Museum in London. (LSE Archives)

because the same relationship that existed between inflation and unemployment in the 1860s also characterized
the relationship between these two variables in the 1950s.
The Phillips curve remained structurally stable for over a
century.

This was a revelation. If unemployment had always been high in the past, when inflation was low, economists argued that this same relationship should hold in the future. If government could influence one of these variables, it could also influence the other. The fact that the Phillips curve was structurally stable was thought to represent a feature of the private economy that represented a constraint on economic policy. Its existence was explained by the Keynesian theory of aggregate supply. If this theory is correct, increased fiscal deficits during the administrations of Presidents Kennedy, Johnson, and Nixon should have restored full employment without causing inflation.

TWO AMERICAN KEYNESIANS

In Keynesian theory, increases in employment come first. Inflation comes second, but only after everyone who wants a job has one. At this point, aggregate demand hits a barrier and continued increases in demand generate increases in money prices. The Keynesians argued that wages are flexible upward but not downward. If aggregate expenditure by government and the private sector on goods and services were subsequently to fall, the money wage would not fall and instead firms would fire workers and the reduction in expenditure would cause a recession.

Two American Nobel Laureates, Paul Samuelson and Robert Solow, summarized the mainstream Keynesian view that evolved from Phillips's article.[4] They phrased the debate as a policy dilemma. If government attempted to control inflation by managing aggregate demand, the economy would face a trade-off. Lower inflation could be obtained at the cost of higher unemployment or lower unemployment at the cost of higher inflation. The government would have to choose which of the two alternatives was preferable.

FIGURE 4.2 Paul A. Samuelson, 1915–2009. Samuelson, who died on December 13, 2009, was an American emeritus professor of economics at the Massachusetts Institute of Technology. He won the Nobel Prize in 1970 "for the scientific work through which he has developed static and dynamic economic theory and actively contributed to raising the level of analysis in economic science." Samuelson had an enormous influence on all branches of economics in the second half of the twentieth century. (Time & Life Pictures/Getty Images)

If government were to stimulate aggregate demand by lowering the interest rate or reducing taxes, it would lower the unemployment rate. But the cost of this policy would be higher inflation. Alternatively, if government were to

FIGURE 4.3 Robert Solow, 1924–present. Solow is an American emeritus professor at the Massachusetts Institute of Technology. He won the Nobel Prize in 1970 "for his contributions to the theory of economic growth." Solow's work forms the basis for the modern neoclassical analysis of growth and development. Along with Paul Samuelson, he is one of the most influential Keynesians. (Donna Coveney/MIT)

reduce aggregate demand by raising taxes or increasing the interest rate, it would reduce inflation at the cost of higher unemployment.

Samuelson and Solow's own work on inflation and unemployment in the United States confirmed that the same relationship held between inflation and unemployment in the U.S. data that Bill Phillips had discovered in the UK data. They interpreted the Phillips curve as a constraint on policy. For them, it was the job of the economist to find out how much inflation would be needed to reduce unemployment by a given amount. It was the job of the policymaker to choose how much unemployment and how much inflation society could tolerate. More of one would inevitably mean less of the other.

THE NATURAL RATE HYPOTHESIS

The Samuelson-Solow interpretation of the Phillips curve did not go unchallenged. In 1968, two influential Nobel Laureates, economists Edmund Phelps of Columbia University and Milton Friedman of the University of Chicago, argued in separate articles that we should not expect to see a permanent long-run relationship between inflation and unemployment. They explained this position by pointing out that the unemployment rate depends on fundamental real factors such as the productivity of workers, the preferences of households, and the time and trouble spent by workers in searching for jobs.[5]

In his 1968 address to the American Economics Association, Friedman introduced the idea of the *natural rate of unemployment*.

> The "natural rate of unemployment," ... is the level that would
> be ground out by the Walrasian system of general equilibrium
> equations, provided there is imbedded in them the actual struc-
> tural characteristics of the labor and commodity markets, includ-
> ing market imperfections, stochastic variability in demands and
> supplies, the cost of gathering information about job vacancies
> and labor availabilities, the costs of mobility, and so on. (Fried-
> man, 1968, p. 8)

Friedman is saying that it is possible to augment general equilibrium theory by adding elements such as the cost of searching for a job, and that the augmented model would be able to explain why there is unemployment. A model that is augmented in this way would not display a long-run

FIGURE 4.4 Edmund S. Phelps Jr., 1937–present. Phelps is an American economist who teaches at Columbia University. He wrote a number of influential papers on economic growth but is best known for being one of two founders (the other was Milton Friedman) of the natural rate hypothesis. Phelps won the Nobel Prize in 2006 "for his analysis of intertemporal trade-offs in macroeconomic policy." (AFP/Getty Images)

trade-off between unemployment and inflation because the factors that determine the unemployment rate have nothing to do with the quantity of money or the rate of inflation. Friedman's argument asserts that Samuelson and Solow were wrong to view the Phillips curve as a trade-off that

FIGURE 4.5 Milton Friedman, 1912–2006. Friedman was an American economist who taught at the University of Chicago. He is known for monetarism, the doctrine that the money supply must be controlled to prevent inflation and promote growth. He won the Nobel Prize in 1976 "for his achievements in the fields of consumption analysis, monetary history and theory and for his demonstration of the complexity of stabilization policy." (Getty Images)

could be exploited by a policymaker to choose either high inflation and low unemployment or low unemployment and high inflation. Instead, he claimed that there is a natural rate of unemployment that is independent of fiscal and monetary policy and is consistent, in the long run, with *any* rate of inflation.

THE BELL TOLLS FOR
BILL PHILLIPS'S CURVE

Phelps and Friedman did not have long to wait before events provided a dramatic confirmation of their thesis. During the 1970s, the U.S. economy experienced high inflation and high unemployment at the same time and the data did not lie anywhere near the Phillips curve that had characterized the relationship between these two variables over the previous century.

In January 1975, unemployment was over 9% and inflation was 13%. An economist who used the Phillips curve to predict inflation would have expected to see prices falling at a rate of 1%, not rising at a rate of 13%. The Phillips curve that had fit so well in the previous century of data was no longer there. It was as if a physicist had used Newton's laws to launch a rocket to the moon and missed by a very wide margin because suddenly the gravitational constant had doubled. The experience was shattering to the Keynesian theory of aggregate supply, and it caused a rupture in the discipline that persists to this day.

The Phillips curve broke down because firms and workers began to increase wages and prices in an inflationary spiral. Wages went up because workers believed that prices would rise. Prices went up because higher wages were passed on to consumers. Inflation worked its way into the psyches of market participants as the upward march of inflation became embedded in self-fulfilling expectations.

At the same time that inflation began to explode, unemployment was high and rising. This could not have occurred if the Phillips curve had remained in place, because it predicted that high inflation can only occur when the economy is operating at full employment.

President Nixon took office in 1969 and by the early 1970s, consumer price inflation was already at 6%. Nixon responded by imposing wage and price controls, but his edicts were about as effective as King Canute's attempt to persuade Neptune to roll back the tides. American corporations became accustomed to raising prices and, correspondingly, American workers asked for higher wages in their contract negotiations. Union contracts accounted for roughly 30% of the workforce at this time and many other wage agreements were formally indexed to inflation, even outside the union sector.

NATURAL RATE THEORY: FACT OR FICTION? . . .

The theory that there is a natural rate of unemployment that is independent of monetary and fiscal policy in the long run is a cornerstone of modern economics. A belief in this theory is widely held by almost all academic and policy economists alive today. The theory is alive and well in the Federal Reserve System as evidenced by the following remarks of Chairman Bernanke, who blamed stagflation on errors of the Fed in estimating the natural rate of unemployment:

> . . . monetary policy makers bemoaned the high rate of inflation in the 1970s but did not fully appreciate their own role in its creation. Ironically, their errors in estimating the natural rate [of unemployment] and in ascribing inflation to nonmonetary forces were mutually reinforcing. (Bernanke, 2004)

According to Bernanke, the Fed was responsible for allowing inflation to build up in the 1970s because it made "errors in estimating the natural rate."

If the natural rate theory is so widely held by economists, one might think that there is strong evidence in its favor. But this is not so. As with any science, economics contains some propositions that cannot easily be tested. This problem is more acute in economics than in the experimental sciences since we are unable to conduct controlled experiments on real economies. In examining the economy, we must be content to explain the data that nature gives us. When that data appear to contradict natural rate theory, an economist who holds strongly to the theory will modify it in a way that restores its consistency with the facts. That is exactly what happened.

In the simplest version of natural rate theory, the natural rate of unemployment is a constant. Beginning with this idea, the Fed, the European Central Bank, and the Bank of England devoted a huge amount of time and effort to estimate its value. They viewed this activity as important because the accepted theory of inflation predicts that an unemployment rate that is less than the natural rate will lead to inflationary pressures that may be difficult to remove.

If the natural rate is constant, then it should be a simple matter to find out its value. One could estimate the natural rate of unemployment by finding the average unemployment rate over many years. But attempts to use this approach failed because researchers quickly discovered that the unemployment rate moves around a lot, not just during booms and recessions, but also between one recession and the next.

... SCIENCE OR RELIGION?

Long-run averages of the unemployment rate vary widely from one decade to the next. The natural rate theorists hold that this is because the natural rate of unemployment changes over time. But unless they are willing to specify in advance exactly how and why it will change, no amount of empirical evidence can be brought to bear to refute this idea.[6]

When the Fed raises the interest rate and causes an increase in unemployment, as it did in 1979, natural rate theorists respond that the economy is temporarily away from its natural rate. When changes in the unemployment rate persist after the recession is over, they say that the natural rate has changed. Perhaps this is true, but it is not good science. As the philosopher of science Karl Popper argued, a scientific theory must be capable of being falsified by some set of facts that we might observe.[7] A theory that cannot be falsified by any set of observable facts is not science; it is religion.

The natural rate hypothesis cannot explain why very high unemployment persists for decades at a time, and it cannot convincingly explain why the natural rate of unemployment may be 10% in one decade and 2% in another.

In my book *Expectations, Employment and Prices*, I provide an alternative theory of movements in the unemployment rate that *can* explain these facts and that is consistent with the main principles of microeconomics. In my work, as in Keynes's *General Theory*, there is no tendency for the economy to converge to a long-run natural rate of unemployment. Instead, the long-run unemployment rate can be anything. It depends on the confidence of participants in the stock market. In chapter 7, I will explain this idea and I will show why the unemployment rate is not pinned down by the assumption that the quantity of labor demanded is equal to the quantity supplied.

CHAPTER 5

The Rational Expectations Revolution

[Macroeconomic theory] . . . has at its base two fundamental postulates. First, individuals act purposefully to achieve the ends they seek. . . . Second, since outcomes depend upon the actions of everyone in society, agents must form expectations about the actions of others, and indeed expectations of the expectations of others, and so on. This feature can be captured by the notion of equilibrium.

—V.V. Chari (1998, p. 172)

V.V. Chari is a leading macroeconomist at the University of Minnesota. In this quote, he is describing the contribution to macroeconomics of Robert E. Lucas Jr., one of five living economic Nobel Laureates at the University of Chicago. Chari concludes with these words: "Robert Lucas is the preeminent macroeconomist of the last 25 years." What did Robert Lucas contribute to macroeconomics and why is it important?

Lucas was the leading figure in the *rational expectations revolution*, a pathbreaking new movement that swept macroeconomics in the 1970s and replaced Keynesian economics with an updated and revised version of classical ideas. Rational expectations economics uses sophisticated mathematics to provide a rigorous foundation to classical theory. It has had a profound effect on the discipline, and the theory of rational expectations dominates the curriculum at all major universities throughout the world today.

Just as classical economics was divided into two parts, so, too, is rational expectations economics. A development of general equilibrium theory called *real business cycle theory* is used to understand how real quantities and relative prices are determined. A development of the quantity theory of money called *new-Keynesian economics* is used to understand how money prices and the rate of inflation are determined. As I will explain later in this chapter, the name adopted by the new-Keynesians is most unfortunate, because their ideas have little to do with Keynes. They have much more in common with the quantity theory of money developed by David Hume.

BOB LUCAS AND ECONOMIC POLICY

When Phelps and Friedman published their work on the natural rate hypothesis in 1968, most economists saw it as a statement about what would happen to the unemployment rate in the long run. They argued that if the Fed were to lower the interest rate, it might lower the unemployment rate over short periods of time of one to two years, but in the long run the unemployment rate would be determined by three fundamentals of the economy: the preferences of households, the stock of skilled and unskilled labor, and the current state of technology.

In 1972, Lucas published an important article in the *Journal of Economic Theory*.[1] He took the arguments of Phelps and Friedman one step further by formalizing their ideas and adding a theory of how people form expectations. Rational expectations is the idea that you can't fool all of the people all of the time. Whatever market participants

FIGURE 5.1 Robert E. Lucas Jr., 1937–present. Lucas is an American economist who teaches at the University of Chicago. He provided a new foundation to macroeconomics. Lucas won the Nobel Prize in 1995, "having developed and applied the hypothesis of rational expectations, and thereby having transformed macroeconomic analysis and deepened our understanding of economic policy." (AP Images/Charles Bennett)

believe about the future must be consistent, on average, with what happens. Lucas's ideas led to the development of real business cycle theory, a movement that replaced Keynesian economics as the dominant approach used by macroeconomists to understand the real economy. It also led to new-Keynesian economics, an extension of real business cycle theory that adds economic frictions to understand the short-run and long-run effects of money on prices and employment. New-Keynesian economics explains why Fed policy influences unemployment first, and inflation much later.

Although Phelps and Friedman believed that the Fed could not alter the unemployment rate in the long run, they still believed that the Fed could improve economic welfare in the short run by lowering the interest rate in a recession. Lucas argued that policymakers cannot improve the welfare of the average citizen through monetary or fiscal policy even in the short run. His theory implied that unemployment can deviate from its natural rate only if households and firms make mistakes in their forecasts of future business conditions.

The rational expectations revolution was a new way of thinking about macroeconomics that swept away Keynesian economics from most academic departments. It was successful because it came at a time when the public had lost faith in Keynesian ideas after economists failed to predict stagflation in the 1970s.

THE FRENCH INFLUENCE

Lucas's work is based on developments of general equilibrium theory by a French-born Nobel Laureate and naturalized American, Gérard Debreu, who spent most of his career in the economics department at Berkeley. He was trained as a mathematician at the École Normale Supérieure in Paris and he brought the rigor of mathematics to general equilibrium theory, as well as a huge amount of insight.

FIGURE 5.2 Gérard Debreu, 1921–2004. Debreu was a French-born economist who taught at the University of California at Berkeley. Although Debreu was a micro-economist, his work on general equilibrium forms the basis of modern macroeconomics. He won the Nobel Prize in 1983 "for having incorporated new analytical methods into economic theory and for his rigorous reformulation of the theory of general equilibrium." (Archives of the Mathematisches Forschungsinstitut Oberwolfach)

In a slim little volume, *Theory of Value*, Debreu took Walras's concept of general equilibrium theory and used modern mathematics to provide very general conditions under which the first welfare theorem of economics is true.[2] Almost as an afterthought, he added a chapter that argued that general equilibrium theory is a great deal more general than usually assumed. By thinking of a commodity as having a date of delivery and a geographical location, he showed that the theory could be used to understand all of trade at all points in time.

This changed everything. For example, according to Walras's version of general equilibrium theory, a loaf of bread is a loaf of bread. In Debreu's version, a loaf of bread is different if it is in a different geographical location or if it is purchased at a different point in time. A loaf of bread purchased at 3:45 in the afternoon in Paris on March 17, 2008, is a different commodity from a loaf of bread purchased at 12:00 noon in Nice on March 18 of the same year.

In an astonishing insight that has been hugely useful to the modern theory of finance, he went one step further. Commodities are different not just because they are delivered on a different date in a different location but also because of differences in random events that may or may not occur. Suppose that the weather in London could be sunny or rainy. An umbrella purchased in London on September 28, 2009, if the sun is shining is a different commodity from an umbrella purchased in the same place at the same time when it's raining. Wall Street uses this idea to price securities by determining their values in terms of the underlying risk associated with any sequence of future payments.

HOW LUCAS CHANGED MACROECONOMICS FOREVER

Lucas used Debreu's insight to change forever the way that macroeconomists think about unemployment. In a brilliant stroke, he threw away Keynesian economics and replaced it with Debreu's version of general equilibrium theory.

When economists before Lucas saw unemployment in the labor market, they thought they were observing a market in disequilibrium. Some prices had not had a chance to adjust to the level that would equate the quantity demanded with the quantity supplied. In this view, the market was not able to establish the right set of equilibrium prices, and as a consequence we often saw households and firms buying and selling commodities at prices that were internally inconsistent. Unemployment occurred because the wage was too high and it had not had time to adjust to its equilibrium level.

By applying Debreu's definition of a commodity, Lucas argued that we *never* see a market in disequilibrium. According to Lucas's new theory, when unemployment goes up or down, it is because the fundamentals of the economy are changing. The prices that we see and the quantities that are traded are always prices for which the quantity demanded is equal to the quantity supplied. The fact that the quantity of labor employed by firms changes over time reflects underlying changes in household preferences for leisure, shocks to the technology of production, or new people entering or leaving the labor force.

Lucas persuaded many academic economists to stop working on Keynesian economics and to switch instead to the study of economic growth.[3] He was successful for two reasons: one empirical and one theoretical. Empirically, Keynesian economics was discredited by the inability of the theory to explain stagflation. Theoretically, Keynesian economics was discredited by an attack on its logical foundations, which were questioned by theorists who pointed to the inconsistency of Keynes's *General Theory* with an established body of microeconomics. Either of these weaknesses alone might have survived a concerted attack by opponents; together they proved fatal.

Lucas's influence on the profession is hard to overestimate. His opinions are far more flexible in personal conversation than in his writing, which contains some of the most persuasive rhetoric written in economics in the past 200 years. I first met him in 1982 when I was a freshly minted Ph.D. teaching at the University of Pennsylvania. He displays an impressive intensity for all things economic, and a willingness to discuss anything about economics with students and professors and to treat them all as intellectual equals, at least until proved otherwise.

REAL BUSINESS CYCLE THEORY

In addition to spurring new research on economic growth, Lucas shaped the way the profession looked at business cycles. He restored general equilibrium theory as the main approach for understanding employment, output, and relative prices and he advanced his view by explicitly modeling the way that households make decisions over time. The general equilibrium theory of Walras dealt with the economy at a point in time. The general equilibrium theory of Lucas dealt with the economy over an entire infinite future and allowed agents to make decisions under uncertainty by taking their best guess as to what events might unfold. The version of general equilibrium theory that was introduced into economics following Lucas is called real business cycle theory.[4]

The most influential figure in the development of real business cycle theory is the Nobel Laureate Edward Prescott. Prescott worked during the late 1970s and 1980s at the University of Minnesota and is currently the W. P. Carey Professor at Arizona State University and a consultant with the Minneapolis Fed. Together with fellow Nobel Laureate Finn Kydland, Prescott extended the methods pioneered by Lucas to describe macroeconomics. Kydland and Prescott first teamed up in 1971 at Carnegie Mellon University, where Kydland was a graduate student and Prescott was a professor. Kydland now teaches at the University of California at Santa Barbara.

FIGURE 5.3 Edward C. Prescott, 1940–present. Prescott is an American economist who teaches at Arizona State University. Along with Finn Kydland, he developed the theory of real business cycles, which describes how shocks to technology can cause recessions. Kydland and Prescott won the Nobel Prize in 2004 "for their contributions to dynamic macroeconomics: the time consistency of economic policy and the driving forces behind business cycles." (AFP/Getty Images)

Prescott is a towering figure in the modern history of economics. His influence on the subject is huge, not just through his writing, but also through his students. The first time I met Ed Prescott, I found our conversation

FIGURE 5.4 Finn Kydland, 1943–present. Kydland is a Norwegian-born economist who teaches at the University of California, Santa Barbara. Kydland was a corecipient of the 2004 Nobel Memorial Prize in Economics (shared with Edward C. Prescott) "for their contributions to dynamic macroeconomics: the time consistency of economic policy and the driving forces behind business cycles." (Getty Images)

incomprehensible. Somewhere in the middle of a sentence he would break off and start a different topic that seemed completely disconnected from anything we were talking about—at least, what I thought we were talking about. But the next time we talked, I realized that a conversation with Ed is unlike any other intellectual experience. It's more like carrying out three or four conversations at the same time, and once you learn to go with the flow, it's an educational opportunity like no other. Ed's students learn this early. Many of them are themselves now leaders in the profession.

Although real business cycle theory is mathematically rigorous, it is simpler than the verbal theories of classical business cycle theory described by Pigou. There is no unemployment in the model, and all variations in employment are voluntary variations in the number of hours that people want to work. This simplification allowed the developers of real business cycle theory to concentrate on what they believed to be its most important aspects: a description of the dynamics of employment, investment, consumption, and GDP that are triggered by changes in productivity that arise from the ebb and flow of new ideas as they impact the economy.

As an example of the kind of shocks emphasized by real business cycle theory, consider the invention of the personal computer. This triggered a movement of workers out of old industries such as steel and automobiles and into high-tech industries that required different skills. During this process, employment fell temporarily but eventually, as new workers were trained, the economy became more productive and new jobs were created. The invention of the personal computer is an example of a shock that has effects that influence employment, consumption, and investment over a period of time, and the study of this process became the new standard for the study of booms and busts.

NEW-KEYNESIAN ECONOMICS

In chapter 2, we saw how classical economics was divided into two parts. General equilibrium theory was used to explain relative prices. The quantity theory of money was used to explain money prices and inflation. The revival of classical economics in the 1970s produced a similar divide. The real business cycle model that developed from Lucas's revival of general equilibrium theory was used to determine relative prices and to explain employment and output. At the same time, a group of economists, who refer to themselves as new-Keynesians, revived the quantity theory of money and used it to explain how the actions of the Fed impact inflation.

New-Keynesian economists are widely employed in central banks around the world and they are influential in many leading universities. The National Bureau of Economic Research is home to a research program in monetary economics, dominated by new-Keynesians, that until very recently was run by David and Christina Romer of the University of California at Berkeley: Christina resigned in November 2008 to become chairperson of the Council of Economic Advisors in the Obama administration. Other influential new-Keynesians include Jordi Galí of Pompeu Fabra University in Barcelona, Mark Gertler of New York University, and Richard Clarida and Michael Woodford of Columbia University.[5]

The new-Keynesians chose that name to differentiate themselves from the new-classical economics of Lucas and Prescott. Lucas showed that monetary and fiscal policy cannot improve welfare, even in the short run. In real business cycle theory, it is costless for firms to change prices and wages. The new-Keynesians added an explicit cost of changing prices. By adding a friction of this kind, they hoped to overturn the new-classical result that policy cannot improve welfare and to show instead how government monetary and fiscal policy can improve people's lives.

Since the time of Hume, economists have known that when money enters the economy, it first affects quantities and only later affects prices. This is widely understood by central bankers today. In 2009, the Fed responded to the recession by pumping money into the economy. This policy was based on new-Keynesian ideas. Initially, the Fed's actions appear to have helped to prevent the recession from turning immediately into a full-fledged depression. But many economists were worried that this additional money would, sooner or later, cause inflation. In the words of Alan Greenspan (2009), former chairman of the Fed,

> ... the short-term dangers of deflation and longer-term dangers of inflation have to be confronted and removed. Excess capacity is temporarily [in June of 2009] suppressing global prices. But I see inflation as the greater future challenge.... Annual price inflation in the US is significantly correlated (with a $3\frac{1}{2}$-year lag) with annual changes in money supply per unit of capacity.

Greenspan was worried about inflation because between September 2008 and March 2009, the Fed doubled its balance sheet by pumping $800 billion of new money into the U.S. economy. Historically, monetary expansion of this kind had led to inflation with a lag of more than three years. As of the summer of 2009, it was unclear whether inflation would reappear.

The way that money influences the economy, first by changing quantities and later by changing prices, is called the monetary transmission mechanism. The formalization of the monetary transmission mechanism using the ideas of the rational expectations revolution is a considerable intellectual achievement. But it doesn't help us understand the Great Depression or the 2008 financial crisis.

QUANTITY THEORISTS IN
KEYNESIAN CLOTHES

But although new-Keynesian economics has much to com-
mend it, new-Keynesian economists do not have much to
say about the Keynes of *The General Theory*. The labor
market in the new-Keynesian model is classical in the sense
that there is no unemployment and every worker chooses
to work as hard as he or she wishes at the market wage.
It is for this reason that the name "new-Keynesian" is a
misnomer, albeit one that has stuck. The new-Keynesians
are in fact quantity theorists in Keynesian clothes, who have
created a sophisticated mathematical formalization of a process whereby an increase in the stock of money first affects
quantities and later affects prices. This is the adjustment
process first described by David Hume.

In the new-Keynesian model, all movements in the
unemployment rate represent small deviations from the rate
that would be chosen by a social planner. In contrast, Keynes
believed that the unemployment rate could differ permanently from the natural rate. The difference is important
because, as I will show in chapter 7, the policies that are
appropriate to reduce unemployment if the natural rate
hypothesis is false are not the same as those described by
the new-Keynesians.

Part of my skepticism of new-Keynesian economics arises
from the difficulty of explaining, in a new-Keynesian model,
why unemployment is so painful. In an influential paper,
Robert Lucas showed that because booms and busts are
efficient in classical models, the average American would be
willing to give up less than one-tenth of 1% of consumption in order to live in a world without variations in the
employment rate. It follows, if the new-Keynesian model is
correct, that we may as well disband the Fed because the use

of fiscal and monetary policy to prevent recessions would be a pointless exercise that costs more in terms of the salaries of government employees than any potential benefit from stabilizing variations in employment and GDP.[6]

Although the new-Keynesians continued to focus on business cycles, they did it using the rules laid down by Lucas, not those of Keynes's *General Theory*. New-Keynesian economic models explain how small frictions move the unemployment rate temporarily away from its natural rate, but they cannot account for large persistent movements in the unemployment rate of the kind that we saw during the Great Depression and they cannot help us through the kind of financial crisis that began in the fall of 2007.

How Central Banks Impact Your Life

All the perplexities, confusion and distress in America arise not from defects in their Constitution or Confederation, nor from want of honor or virtue, so much as downright ignorance of the nature of coin, credit, and circulation.

—John Adams (2nd U.S. president, 1787, in a letter to Thomas Jefferson)

The amount of money flowing around a modern economy is regulated by a nation's central bank. In the UK, this is the Bank of England; in Europe, it is the European Central Bank; and in the United States, it is the Federal Reserve System, a network of 12 banks scattered around the country with headquarters at the Board of Governors based in Washington, DC.

In the spring of 2009, the activities of central banks were at the forefront of the news. Mervyn King, governor of the Bank of England, was involved in public disputes with Alistair Darling, the UK chancellor of the exchequer. Jean-Claude Trichet, president of the European Central Bank; Ben Bernanke, chairman of the Fed; and Mervyn King, governor of the Bank of England, were major players in the response to the global credit crisis that began in 2007.

Although this chapter will use the U.S. central bank as an example, everything I will say about the Fed has parallels with central banks in every country in the world. How do the decisions taken by central banks affect our everyday lives?

It is sometimes said that the chairman of the Federal Reserve System is the second most powerful person in the world, after the U.S. president, and there is some truth to this statement. The chairman of the Fed has the power to influence monetary policy and to set interest rates. If the Fed makes the wrong decision, millions of people could lose their jobs, inflation rates could spiral out of control, or the value of the stock market could plummet. All of these things can and have happened in the United States since the creation of the Fed in 1913, and all of them have been attributed by one or more commentators to the mistakes of the Fed.

From 1987 through 2006, the Fed was chaired by Alan Greenspan. A devotee of the free market philosopher Ayn Rand, Greenspan was celebrated in the 1990s as an economic wizard and was thought by some to be the most successful Fed chairman ever. When major U.S. financial institutions began to collapse in the fall of 2008, many commentators began to revise their opinion as people looked for someone to blame for what many saw as an impending economic meltdown. Greenspan probably does not deserve all the credit for the remarkable economic expansion of the 1990s—nor does he deserve all of the blame for the collapse of the economy that started in 2007. The truth lies somewhere in between.

WHO OWNS THE FED?

The Fed was created in 1913. It is a nonprofit-making institution, accountable to Congress, and is, in effect, an independent arm of the U.S. government. The Fed is financed from interest earned on its assets, which until recently consisted primarily of Treasury bills issued by the U.S. government. Any revenues it earns that exceed its operating costs are returned to the U.S. Treasury.[1]

The Fed is managed by a seven-member board of governors, appointed by the president and confirmed by the U.S. Senate, and although the members of the board are political appointees, they serve for overlapping 14-year terms and once appointed cannot be removed from office. This gives the Fed a fair amount of autonomy from any given political administration, since individual appointees serve terms that may span several administrations.

The primary role of the Fed is to manage the nation's money supply. Before 1933, this process was automatic, because the quantity of money was determined by flows of precious metals into and out of the country in response to changes in export and import flows. During this period, the United States was on the *gold standard* and it was possible for both Americans and foreigners to exchange U.S. dollars for gold at a fixed rate. A dollar bill represented a title to a fixed weight of gold bullion. After 1933, U.S. citizens were no longer able to exchange a U.S. dollar for gold and the dollar became a purely paper promise backed by nothing other than faith in the U.S. government.[2] At one time a dollar could be exchanged for a fixed weight of gold. Now it can be exchanged for an identical piece of paper.

MONEY MAKES THE WORLD GO AROUND

The oldest central bank in the world is the "Old Lady of Threadneedle Street," a nickname for the Bank of England, which was founded in 1694 to act as the government's banker and debt manager. The newest is the European Central Bank, which was founded in 1998 with the creation of the new European currency, the euro. The euro, as of 2009, was the official currency of 16 of the 27 member states of the European Union, and it is used daily by some 327 million Europeans.

Money consists not only of pound notes, dollar bills, or euros in circulation but also of checkable deposits that can be used for transactions. The nation's central bank alters the amount of money in circulation by expanding or contracting the amount of domestic credit, and since every new loan creates a new bank account, the expansion of credit leads to an expansion of deposits that are good substitutes for bank notes.

The operational details of monetary policy vary from country to country, but the effect is the same. In the United States, the expansion or contraction of credit is achieved through *open market operations*, which come under the direction of the policy arm of the Fed—the open market committee. The open market committee meets eight times a year and its main policy instrument is the federal funds rate—the interest rate charged on overnight loans between banks. The Fed influences this rate by buying or selling Treasury bills on the open market.

THE MODERN FED

The era of modern monetary policy began in 1951 when the Treasury and the Fed signed an agreement, *the Accord*, which gave the Fed significant autonomy in setting the interest rate. During the Great Depression, the interest rate on short-term Treasury bills had been a fraction of a percentage point and it had remained at less than a half a percentage point throughout World War II. This was a direct result of a policy in which the Fed agreed to keep down the cost of borrowing by the Treasury to finance the war. The Accord freed the Fed from this obligation to the Treasury and gave it a significant new freedom—the power to choose monetary policy independently of political influence.[3]

Initially, the Treasury was resistant to allowing the Fed this new freedom. Government debt as a fraction of GDP had trebled from 40% of GDP in 1938 to 120% in 1946, and the Treasury would have preferred to keep the interest rate low to reduce the cost to the federal government of running additional deficits. But the Fed argued persuasively that their hand was forced by market pressure. Although it might be possible to keep the interest rate low on three-month Treasury bills, the interest rate on longer-term bonds had already begun to increase. The interest rate on longer-term securities contains a premium for inflation, and by 1951, the markets were demanding an increased inflation premium to safeguard lenders against the impact of higher expected future prices. In 1951, the Treasury wanted the Fed to finance its expenditure by printing money. The Fed was concerned that this would lead to inflation, and ultimately, they were shown to be correct.

Some economists were concerned in the summer of 2009 that the Fed policy of buying up long-term government debt was beginning to have the same effect on the bond markets as it had in the 1950s and 1960s. In mid-December 2008, yields on long-term Treasury bonds were just above 2%. By June, they had climbed to almost 4%. Are we in for a repeat of the slow inflation buildup of the earlier years? Some influential economists, including past Fed chairman Alan Greenspan, see this as a distinct possibility. Writing in the *Financial Times*, Greenspan argued that "If political pressures prevent central banks from reining in their inflated balance sheets in a timely manner, statistical analysis suggests the emergence of inflation by 2012."[4]

FIGHTING INFLATION

The job of the Fed chairman is, at times, like that of a fireman in a burning building. In one room is a baby in a crib; in another is an unconscious mother. The fireman can save one but not the other, and whichever decision he makes, he will be blamed by somebody for making the wrong one.

The Fed can choose to fight the recession by lowering the interest rate, but since recessions are temporary, this policy is one that generates only short-term gains. When the Fed lowers the interest rate to stimulate the economy in a recession, it may feed inflationary expectations. As the

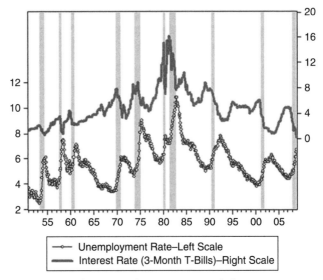

FIGURE 6.1 The unemployment rate and the interest rate. Shaded regions are NBER recessions.

olcker took control as
the Fed was much less
in response to inflation
tion, and interest rates
after 1979 than before.
at Moderation.
ributed the Great Mod-
conduct of monetary
e Fed simply got lucky
omy in the later period
sue, economists turned
niversity professor John

war period, the behavior
by a simple mechanical
e in response to increased
to increased unemploy-
le were different before
Paul Volcker took over
y policy became more
te during business cycle

f Columbia University,
niversity in Barcleona,
University used new-
now that the change in
for improved economic
of Princeton University
ve Bank of Atlanta used
nstead that the Fed was
was lower after 1979 than
t is perhaps unsurprising
etation, which paints the
g central bankers. But in

economy emerges from the recession, it does so at the cost of permanently higher inflation. This is what happened in the period from 1951 through 1982, as after every recession the inflation rate crept a little higher. Higher inflation went hand in hand with higher interest rates, and by 1981, the interest rate on a 30-year fixed-rate mortgage was over 18% per year.

The effect on first-time home buyers was catastrophic. A GI returning from World War II would have paid $59 a month in interest and principal for every $10,000 dollars that he borrowed. By 1981, his children would be paying $150 for the same loan.

FIGHTING UNEMPLOYMENT

Figure 6.1 illustrates the history of the U.S. unemployment rate and the interest rate from 1951 through 2008. The unemployment rate is the line marked by circles and is measured on the left axis. The interest rate is the solid line measured on the right axis. The shaded regions are recessions defined by the Business Cycle Dating Committee of the National Bureau of Economic Research.

Including the current recession, which began in December 2007, there have been 10 recessions since 1951. The figure illustrates clearly that every one of them was associated with a sharp increase in the unemployment rate and at the same time a sharp reduction in the interest rate on Treasury bills. In each recession, the interest rate fell because the Fed was trying to alleviate the adverse effects of the recession on people's lives.

The Fed cannot simply use the interest rate as a tool to control recessions; it must also pay attention to inflation. In the period before 1979, it did not pay sufficient attention to that dimension of policy. Figure 6.2 shows the history of

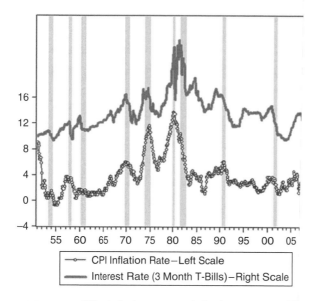

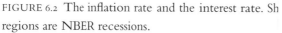

FIGURE 6.2 The inflation rate and the interest rate. Sh
regions are NBER recessions.

inflation (the line marked by circles, measured o
axis) and the interest rate (the solid line measure
right axis).[5]

Although the Fed lowered the interest rate duri
sions, it allowed it to increase during expansions. I
shows that, beginning with the end of the Korea
1953, there was a steady buildup of inflation from
0% in August 1955 to a peak of 13.7% in March 1(
1980, inflation came down rapidly and has stayed
since.

WHY INFLATION MATTERS

Inflation isn't bad for everyone. It redistributes
from savers to borrowers. Consider a typical 196

beginning in 1979, when P
chairman of the Fed. Before
aggressive in raising the intere
than after. Economic growth
were lower and much less vc
Economists call this change th

Some economic theorists h.
eration to an improvement i
policy. Others have claimed t
since the shocks that hit the
were less severe. To decide t
to empirical work by Stanfo
Taylor.

Taylor showed that over the
of the Fed can be mimicked
rule. The Fed raised the interes
inflation and lowered it in resp
ment. The characteristics of th
and after 1979. After 1979, w
as chairman of the Fed, mor
aggressive in raising the intere
expansions than before.[6]

Economists Richard Clarid
Jordi Galí of Pompeu Fabra
and Mark Gertler of New Y
Keynesian economic theory t
policy may have been responsi
performance.[7] Christopher Si
and Tao Zha of the Federal R
econometric methods to argu
lucky and the volatility of shoc
before.[8] This debate is ongoing
that Clarida-Galí-Gertler's inte
Fed as the hero, is popular am

2008, when the economy was teetering on the brink of depression, a story that praised the success of monetary policy seemed sadly lacking.

THE ROLE OF GOOD LUCK

The argument that the Great Moderation can be attributed to an improvement in the policy of the Fed is largely correct. But it misses an important part of the puzzle. The Fed did learn how to move the interest rate more effectively to prevent inflation—but it was also lucky.

The period from 1979 to 2006 was one in which there were few major shocks to the real economy. Although there was a big shock to confidence when the stock market crashed in 1987, it was quickly restored by Alan Greenspan, who called together the heads of the major Wall Street investment banks and guaranteed to lend them unlimited amounts of money until the crisis was averted and the stock market had recovered.[9]

The fact that the Fed managed to restore confidence to the markets in 1987 was, in my view, as much good luck as good policy. If confidence had not been restored, the effects of the 1987 crash on the real economy would have been much closer to those of 1929 or 2008. The Fed was lucky in 1987 because its actions restored confidence in the markets and private investors put money back into the stock market. It may not be so lucky in the future financial crisis that *will* inevitably reappear.

Modern classical economists insist that confidence cannot independently influence the economy. It must be determined by fundamental features of the economy as part of what Robert Lucas called a rational expectations equilibrium.[10] When we make guesses about what the stock market will be worth in the future, the only factors we can consider from this perspective are fundamental features of the economy such as the productivity of technology, the tastes of consumers, or the taxes that will be levied by future governments. The fads and fashions of sentiment that determine consumer and producer confidence are ruled out by assumption. The idea that only fundamentals matter is difficult to reconcile with the swings we observe in the value of stocks because stock market prices move too much to be attributed solely to changes in future fundamentals.

MINSKY MOMENTS

The economist Hyman Minsky presents an alternative to the classical view.[11] According to Minsky's view, the natural state of an economic system is one of recurrent expansions and crashes that are characterized by credit crises. A Minsky moment is the point when the house of cards comes tumbling down and the economy moves from boom to crash. In my view, Minsky's view of how the economy works is much closer to the truth than the classical vision: But Minsky, who was a follower of Keynes, never reconciled Keynesian ideas with classical economic theory. This reconciliation is important because classical theory contains many important truths.

I believe that it *is* possible to understand why the stock market behaves so erratically. It is because, as Keynes asserted, there are many possible long-run equilibrium unemployment rates and all of them are consistent with free markets and rational behavior by individuals. Investors are not irrational; they are undecided about which path will be chosen by future investors, and in my work, I have put these ideas together in an internally coherent way.

Contrary to the assertions of the classical school, I believe that the unemployment rate does not fluctuate around a fixed natural rate—it fluctuates around a moving target, which can be influenced by the policy actions of the Fed. Movements in the unemployment rate are caused by movements in the stock market that are driven by swings in confidence. To fully understand what happens during these swings, we must understand how the wild movements of markets are individually rational even if they are irrational from the viewpoint of society. That was the goal of the research I summarize in my (1993) book that reconciles rational expectations with confidence as an independent driving force of the business cycle. It is, however, an explanation that is missing from the work of Minsky and, as a consequence, an analysis of the current crisis that is based on Minsky's ideas will, I believe, lead us to the wrong policy conclusions.

IN DEFENSE OF CENTRAL BANKS

The ignorance of the role of money and credit that my introductory quote from John Adams alluded to is still with us today. In 2008, I attended a dinner party at the house of a friend. The guests included academics, writers, and movie producers. At one point, the topic of conversation drifted to the role of the Fed and I was surprised to find that more than one of the guests held firmly to the view that the Fed is a conspiracy of East Coast bankers designed to rob honest working Americans of their hard-earned wealth. Since I place opinions like this in the same category as the abduction of one's spouse by aliens or the spontaneous combustion of a dinner guest, the notion that a Fed conspiracy theory could be held by otherwise rational adults was disturbing to me. But it is a view that will be harder to dispel in the current climate, where the financial system has imploded and everyone is looking for someone to blame.

The truth is that, without the Fed controlling the interest rate, the economic history of the twentieth century might have been a great deal more catastrophic than it was. During the nineteenth century, the United States experienced five separate financial crises. In the twentieth century, there was one. Since its inception, in 1913, the Fed has been learning how to control the economy by raising and lowering the interest rate in an effort to prevent inflation and stop depressions. The fact that post–World War II business cycles were much less erratic than prewar cycles suggests that the Fed was successful.

In the first part of the twentieth century, the Fed was still learning how to operate. After World War II, it learned how to curb recessions, and after 1980, it figured out how to do this without fueling inflation. But in spite of these successes, there were two major failures: one in 1929 and the other in 2008. In both cases, the interest rate was already at zero and could not be lowered any further. The Fed did not cause the financial crisis of 2008, and if the interest rate was not already at zero, a policy of lowering the interest rate might have prevented it. It was the impotence of traditional monetary policy, caused by reaching the zero interest rate lower bound, that caused the Great Depression to be so deep and that exacerbated the financial crisis of 2008. The Fed did not cause the crisis, but it was impotent to prevent it.

THE FUTURE OF CENTRAL BANKING

Milton Friedman asserted that long-run Fed policy should concentrate on price stability and that it can only reduce unemployment in the short run at the cost of increasing inflation in the long run. As long as the Fed restricts itself to the interest rate as its only policy instrument, Friedman is correct. But what if there were another demand-management tool that allowed the Fed to change the long-run unemployment rate?

I believe that this tool exists—direct central bank intervention in the stock market to prevent bubbles and crashes by changing the composition of the central bank balance sheet. A second tool of this kind would provide a way of managing the long-run unemployment rate. This instrument is distinct from the primary tool of interest rate control that is used by central banks throughout the world to manage inflation. I will return to this idea in chapter 11, where I will discuss the practical aspects of implementing the management of aggregate stock market wealth.

Established economic theory teaches us that the long-run unemployment rate is independent of aggregate demand. I believe that this established theory is false and that the doctrine of the natural rate of unemployment persists because of the difficulty in economics of conducting a controlled experiment. It is only when large natural experiments are conducted for us, such as the stock market crash of 1929 or the financial crisis of 2008, that obvious deficiencies of classical theory become apparent.

Decades of training in classical economics have blinded our best and brightest minds to the fact that the long-run unemployment rate is not independent of aggregate demand. High unemployment is an inefficient waste of resources that reflects a failure of the market system, and the restoration and maintenance of full employment requires collective action in the form a well-designed government policy. The following chapters explain why the free market sometimes fails and, when it fails, how to fix it.

Why Unemployment Persists

No great improvements in the lot of mankind are possible, until a great change takes place in the fundamental constitution of their modes of thought.

—John Stuart Mill (1824, chapter 7)

The classical economists viewed the economy as a well-oiled machine. Keynes rejected this metaphor because it could not explain the immense human misery that occurred during the Great Depression: But Keynesian economics was itself abandoned in the 1970s when it, too, failed an important empirical test. Keynesian economics could not explain stagflation. The history of economic thought is the history of the response of ideas to important transformational events, and I believe that the financial crisis that began in the fall of 2007 will be another such turning point.

Classical ideas were revived in the 1970s by the rational expectations economists Robert Lucas and Edward Prescott. Although the methods that Lucas and Prescott introduced were revolutionary, the models in which they were first applied were much simpler than the rich verbal theories of the 1920s theorists such as Pigou. Some contemporary critics have responded to the 2008 crash by rushing to tear up rational expectations economics. This response is destructive, unnecessary, and premature.

How *should* economists respond to the financial crisis of 2008, an event that looks to be as disruptive to the rational expectations school as the Great Depression was to the classical theories of the 1920s? I do not believe that we should throw away the progress of the past 35 years. The methods that Lucas and Prescott introduced into economics were just that, mathematical tools that can be used in different ways. The time has come to apply these tools to the insights of Keynes. Just because the real business cycle model that Kydland and Prescott introduced cannot explain financial crises, it does not mean that we should give up on the remarkable new methods of the rational expectations revolution. Instead, we should use them to formalize Keynesian insights. This chapter shows how.

PUTTING UNEMPLOYMENT BACK INTO THE CLASSICAL MODEL

I am going to describe a research agenda, called *search theory*, developed by classical economists to understand why some workers are unemployed. An excellent technical survey of this literature can be found in the (1990) book by Christopher Pissarides of the London School of Economics. Other prominent researchers who made early and influential contributions to the field include Armen Alchian and John McCall of UCLA, Dale Mortensen of Northwestern University, and Peter Diamond of the Massachusetts Institute of Technology.[1]

Search theory began in the 1970s as a way of understanding the natural rate of unemployment. Many of the researchers who worked on this topic wanted to formalize Friedman's idea that the natural rate of unemployment "is the level that would be ground out by the Walrasian system of general equilibrium equations" once "market imperfections" had been properly accounted for.

In layperson's terms, they wanted to introduce unemployment into general equilibrium theory in a way that preserved Pareto's idea that the free market works well. The first welfare theorem might not hold exactly, because of market frictions, but as a first approximation, a market economy with some unemployment should work a lot like the market economy of Walras.

The research program to develop a theory of job search was developed independently from real business cycle theory and, although there were attempts to marry the two, these attempts are generally perceived to have been unsuccessful.

WHY THIS DIDN'T WORK:
SHIMER'S PUZZLE

Robert Shimer of the University of Chicago pointed to a problem that must be addressed by economists who are trying to integrate search theory with real business cycle theory. When these two theories are combined, unemployment in the hybrid model does not move nearly enough during recessions to explain the facts. Unemployment in the data is 10 times more volatile than the unemployment predicted by the theory.[2]

The real business cycle model does a very good job of understanding normal boom-and-bust cycles. For example, it explains why investment falls more than GDP during recessions and why they both move down more than consumption. The theory also gets the magnitudes of these movements right. But when unemployment is added to the model, something goes very wrong.

It's as if an astronomer had a theory that could perfectly explain the orbits of Mars, Saturn, and Jupiter but, when the theory was applied to Earth, it was off by a factor of 10. This suggests that the search theorists are on the wrong track. I believe that the problem with their approach is that classical theorists have built models where, even though workers must search for jobs, the economy is still able to approximate the full employment solution that would be chosen by a social planner. Instead of building models that replicate the invisible hand, we should use the search framework to show how any unemployment rate can persist. Let's see how that might work.

IS UNEMPLOYMENT OPTIMAL?

Most classical theorists use search theory to understand employment in the same way that they use the theory of demand and supply to understand how many oranges will be produced in Florida. Just as there is only one point at which demand and supply are equal in the market for oranges, so, too, there should be only one way in which a competitive market could allocate workers between jobs. In most, but not all, of the models that classical theorists have constructed, the unemployment rate coincides with, or is very close to, the one that would be chosen by a planner with perfect knowledge who acts to maximize the welfare of the people.[3]

It seems hard to believe that the unemployment rate in 2008–2009 in the United States is the one that would be chosen by a social planner. Unemployment in 2009 reached 9.5% in June and was still rising. During the Great Depression, it went above 24%. If the first welfare theorem is true, then a social planner would also have chosen an unemployment rate of 24% during the Great

Depression because technological constraints temporarily changed in a way that made this the right way to satisfy human wants. Even classical economists such as Milton Friedman, who revered free markets, found it difficult to make this argument about unemployment during the Great Depression.

Friedman claimed instead that government failed to provide enough liquidity during the late 1920s and that bad monetary policy had distorted efficient outcomes. According to this view, government is not the solution. It is the problem.[4] But although there is much to be said for the argument that government sometimes does more harm than good, there is also much to be said for the argument that free markets do not always deliver efficient outcomes.

SAND IN THE OIL

How do workers find jobs? The answer is not as obvious as it seems. To answer it, we must think hard about the time and effort that must be expended by workers and firms to find each other.

A job must be produced from inputs, just like any other commodity. Like a car that is produced from capital and labor, a job is produced from the time spent searching for each other by a firm and a worker. The physical description of this process is called the search technology. Although the production technology and the search technology are similar

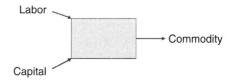

FIGURE 7.1 Producing a commodity.

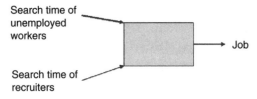

FIGURE 7.2 Producing a job.

(see Figures 7.1 and 7.2), the inputs to the search technology are not like labor and capital. They are different because each of them is a commodity that one side of the market has more information about than the other.

Figure 7.1 illustrates the production process for a good. The inputs are capital and labor. Workers operate machines and add value to raw materials. The output is a good such as a car, a computer, or a can of beans.

Figure 7.2 illustrates the production process for a job. The inputs are the search time of an unemployed worker and the search time of a recruiter in the personnel department of a firm. The recruiters sort through applications of unemployed workers and filter out those who are suitable for vacant jobs. Unemployed workers fill out applications and attend job interviews. The output is a match between an unemployed worker and a vacant position.

General equilibrium theory predicts that the search technology should be run by headhunting firms. Consider an example where the ABC employment agency matches workers with jobs. How would this work? The ABC employment agency should buy the rights to match unemployed workers and vacant jobs from households and firms and put together workers and firms in the same way a computer dating service matches lonely hearts. Once the ABC company has established that Maynard Jagger, an unemployed welder, would fit well with the vacant position at the Detroit Auto Corporation, Detroit Auto Corporation should offer the job to Maynard and pay ABC for the information that he is the best fit.

WHY SEARCH MARKETS DON'T WORK WELL

Why don't private headhunting firms spring into existence to find jobs for unemployed workers? Although we do see some headhunting firms, they are a small fraction of the employment market, and they do not operate in the way that classical economic theory suggests they should. They operate as personnel departments for firms that are too small or too specialized to run their own operations. But they do not pay workers and firms for the right to match them because the markets for search inputs do not exist. It is not hard to see why.

How would these markets operate if they *did* exist? A dishonest unemployed worker could turn down every job he or she was offered and continue to receive payments while remaining unemployed. Since there will often be good reasons to refuse a job, it would be impossible to write a contract in which the worker must take any job that he or she is offered.

In some countries there are organized employment exchanges, run by the government, that pay benefits to unemployed workers. The UK is an example. These institutions often lead to fraud, in which individuals sign up for benefits under multiple names and turn down every job. This kind of behavior leads to the failure of the market. Because market participants have asymmetric information, the headhunting firms predicted by general equilibrium theory do not exist.[5]

WHY HIGH UNEMPLOYMENT EXISTS

A given number of jobs can be filled by a large number of unemployed workers and a few recruiters or by a few unemployed workers and a large number of recruiters. But should society match workers with jobs by asking a few unemployed workers to search for a lot of vacant positions or a lot of unemployed workers to search for a few vacant positions? Either outcome can occur in the real world because the price signals that should tell firms and workers how to behave are missing.

Suppose that a farmer needs to plow a field. He could use one man and a tractor or 20 men, each with a hoe. The first alternative uses a large quantity of capital and a small quantity of labor, and the second uses a large quantity of labor and a small quantity of capital. In a market economy, the rental price of capital and the wage will adjust to ensure that the farmer chooses the right combination of labor and capital given the relative scarcity of the two inputs.

The example of firms searching for workers is different from the example of a farmer plowing a field because there are no markets for search inputs and no prices to direct individual firms and workers on how best to allocate their time. Each firm will allocate more personnel to recruiting if there are very few unemployed workers, and fewer personnel to recruiting if there are many unemployed workers.

Economists say that any unemployment rate is an *equilibrium*, by which they mean that there are no forces acting to change the unemployment rate and that, as a consequence, very high unemployment can persist for a very long time.

WHY THE WAGE DOESN'T FALL

Keynesian economics is often criticized because Keynesians can't explain why, when there are many unemployed people, the wage does not fall to restore equality between the quantity of labor demanded and the quantity supplied. Surely these unemployed people could offer to work for a lower wage than existing workers. It would be in the interest of a firm to hire an unemployed worker because it would be able to make a profit from the transaction. But this argument doesn't take account of the costs of matching a worker with a vacant job.

If a firm were to advertise a job in the newspaper with a lower wage than that offered by other firms, a searching unemployed worker would apply instead for one of the higher paid positions at a rival firm. If the firm were to reallocate its workforce away from production and toward recruiting in order to hire additional workers, the firm would not be able to produce and sell enough commodities to survive at the market wage. The high unemployment situation is an *equilibrium* in which no worker and no firm can profit by changing individual behavior.

Many unemployed workers looking for a job is like many fishermen in a common pond. When there are many other fishermen, it becomes harder for each one to catch a fish. Because no one owns the pond, there is no price signal to tell some of the fishermen to leave. The job search process is like this. There is no price signal to tell some firms to put more or fewer resources into recruiting, and the market sometimes gets the allocation between vacancies and unemployment very wrong. The behavior of other firms in the economy makes each individual firm more or less productive.

In the fall of 2008, the three major U.S. automakers faced tough times. Demand for automobiles had fallen dramatically; GM responded by cutting 15% of its salaried workforce, approximately 5,000 white-collar jobs in the last two months of 2008. Many of these salaried workers were from the personnel department. They were no longer needed because GM responded to decreased sales by producing fewer cars. The net response was a smaller, leaner auto industry with higher productivity and higher real wages. This is exactly what happened to manufacturing industries in the first three years of the Great Depression.[6]

CLASSICAL AND KEYNESIAN USES OF SEARCH THEORY

A huge literature has developed over the past 35 years that builds on a book by Edmund Phelps that was published in 1970. It uses search theory to explain the determinants of the natural rate of unemployment. What is different about this literature from the ideas I have described in this chapter?

When a classically trained economist writes down a model in which a market is missing, his immediate instinct is that the model is incomplete. He must add an equation to show how the unemployment rate is, after all, determined by fundamentals—the preferences of households, the number of skilled and unskilled workers, and the state of technology. Some classical search theorists complete their model by adding a new equation to determine the wage through bargaining. Others introduce fictional "market makers" who compete with each other to match workers with jobs. The goal of classical search theory is to find an extra equation to replace the price signals that are missing in the labor market because of the information problem when some workers may be dishonest.

In my view, most classically trained search theorists have been asking the wrong question. We should not be looking for hidden mechanisms that make the labor market work well. We should instead recognize that these mechanisms are absent, and as a consequence there may be many equilibrium unemployment rates, most of which have very bad welfare consequences. It is because the labor market does not work well that the Great Depression lasted for 10 years in the United States, Japan lost a decade of output in the 1990s, and the UK suffered almost 20 years of anemic growth and high unemployment in the 1920s and 1930s.

Keynes claimed that any unemployment rate could persist as a long-run equilibrium. But he did not explain how long-run unemployment could be consistent with the behavior of rational goal-oriented individuals pursuing their individual self-interests in markets. The postwar Keynesians developed a way of explaining some of Keynes's ideas, but watered them down. In the postwar neoclassical synthesis of Paul Samuelson, unemployment is a temporary phenomenon.

In this chapter, I showed how to integrate Keynes with general equilibrium theory in a new and different way. In my theory, long-run persistent high unemployment is fully consistent with the classical idea of rational behavior in markets. This is important because, as we will see, it suggests a very different policy to cure the problem of high unemployment from the one advocated by Keynesians in the Obama administration in the United States, the Sarkozy government in France, or Gordon Brown's policies in the UK.

If any unemployment rate can persist forever, then what determines which unemployment rate actually occurs? The following chapter answers this question by showing how the labor market is connected to the stock market. I will show that low confidence can result in low asset prices and that a lack of confidence can become a self-fulfilling prophecy that leads to very high unemployment, potentially for a very long period of time.

CHAPTER 8

Why the Stock Market Matters to You

There is always a prevailing bias [in markets]. I'll call it, you know, optimism/pessimism. And sometimes those moods actually can reinforce themselves so that there are these initially self-reinforcing but eventually unsustainable and self-defeating boom/bust sequences or bubbles. And this is what has happened now.

—George Soros (October 10, 2008).

Classical economists argue that the market price of a stock is equal to the sum of the values of the dividends that will be paid to the owner of the stock over the life of the company. According to this theory, called the efficient markets hypothesis, dividends that are paid next month are worth more than dividends in the distant future. Because dividends depend only on market fundamentals, there is no room in the efficient markets hypothesis for market psychology.

Market practitioners know otherwise. The quote that opens this chapter is from the businessman and speculator George Soros, who made his reputation in 1992 when he made more than a billion dollars betting that the UK government would not be able to defend a fixed exchange rate for the pound. Soros is not a market fundamentalist.

He is not alone. Writing in the *Financial Times*, former Fed chairman Alan Greenspan put it like this,

> ... a significant driver of stock prices is the innate human propensity to swing between euphoria and fear, which, while heavily influenced by economic events, has a life of its own. In my experience, such episodes are often not mere forecasts of future business activity, but major causes of it. (Greenspan, 2009)

If market practitioners recognize that confidence drives markets, why is this simple fact not recognized by academic economists? It is because classical economics, a theory that can successfully explain many features of real-world markets, has no room for market psychology. Keynesian economics does. But most macroeconomists gave up on Keynesian economics when it failed to explain stagflation in the 1970s. Any successful rehabilitation of Keynesian ideas must show how confidence drives the markets. This chapter shows how to do that in a way that is fully consistent with neoclassical assumptions about rational behavior by individuals.

DO FUNDAMENTALS DRIVE MARKETS?

Classical economists argue that the value of the stock market is determined by fundamentals. According to this view, if Microsoft shares drop in value, it is because rational investors anticipate that Microsoft's profits will fall. Perhaps there is a new competitor in the market. Perhaps there is a new invention that makes the personal computer obsolete. All market movements arise from rational investors anticipating changes in future fundamentals, and there is no room for the confidence of stock market participants to independently influence economic activity.

For nearly 70 years, investment advisors recommended the wise strategy of investing in the stock market for the long haul. Stocks had outperformed bonds by almost 5% on average over every 10-year period since records began. But in 2008, markets worldwide lost 40% of their value for no sound fundamental reason, and suddenly the premium on stocks made sense as 30 years of capital gains were wiped out overnight. Financial journalists declared that the 2008 crash was the death knell of the efficient markets hypothesis.[1]

... OR DOES CONFIDENCE DRIVE MARKETS?

Keynes argued that most people do not buy and sell shares for the long haul. They buy and sell shares because they think that other people will value them more or less in the future. And what applies to stocks and shares also applies to real estate.

A good example of the get-rich-quick philosophy that dominated popular culture in the late 1990s and early 2000s is the U.S. television show "Flip This House," which encouraged people to speculate in real estate by buying a property, giving it a coat of paint, and selling it quickly for a profit. A blurb from the A&E network puts it like this:

> Tackling one of the most exciting aspects of today's high-stakes real estate market—the transformation of an eyesore into a profit-making beauty—A&E's hour-long "docu-soap" follows the travails of real-estate investors in New Haven, CT, Los Angeles, CA, San Antonio, TX, and Atlanta, GA—where each boasts a team of characters that buys homes, renovates them in record time, then flips them for a profit. It sounds simple, but sparks

fly and tempers are high before the fixer-uppers are ready to go back on the market. (Promotional material from the Arts and Entertainment Television Website: Flip This House[2])

Buyers and sellers of real estate made a lot of money in the first part of the 2000s. But what goes up can also come down. When pessimism sets in, investors undervalue assets such as stocks and houses. If their collective pessimism persists, it reduces wealth and forces a reduction of aggregate demand. New retirees live in smaller houses, buy cheaper cars, and purchase fewer restaurant meals. Young households who are saving for college cut back on spending to replenish their savings. This leads to a vicious cycle that causes firms to lay off workers and profits to fall. As dividends, profits, and investments go down, the initial pessimistic view of the future becomes self-fulfilling.

WHO IS RIGHT?

According to the classical theory, asset prices are determined by rational expectations of future fundamentals. The value of a share in a company is the sum of the values of all of the future dividends that it will pay, weighted by a price that depends on when the dividend will be paid.

According to Keynesian economists, the stock market is driven by confidence. They point to the fact that stock market prices go up and down much more than they should according to classical theory. Dividend payments are much too smooth to justify the movements in stock market prices that we observe.[3] Who is right about the way the stock market works, the classical or the Keynesian economists?

I believe that they are both right and that there is a way of reconciling the fundamentalist and the Keynesian view of the stock market. Classical economists insist that fundamentals drive the market. Keynesians insist that confidence matters. Once we recognize that confidence is a separate independent fundamental just like preferences, endowments, and technology, we can reconcile both points of view. This is not just a trick of language; by insisting that confidence should be treated as a fundamental, I am also insisting that as economists, we maintain the rational expectations view that market participants are not consistently fooled.

Using the classical definition of fundamentals, classical theory is incomplete. Because there is no unique fundamental labor market equilibrium, there is also no unique fundamental value for the price of a stock. By adding confidence as a separate fundamental, we can retain a theory in which everything is determined by fundamentals, including the value of stock prices. Confidence is an independent fundamental driving force of the business cycle.

SWINGS IN CONFIDENCE ARE RATIONAL

How can we reconcile the idea of confidence as a fundamental with the classical idea that rational people take actions that are in their own best interests? Keynes's answer was that the future is not predictable. There is no *right* way to form a belief about the future. He did not try to reconcile this idea with classical economics because his first concern was to influence the contemporary policy debate.

In previous joint work with Jess Benhabib of New York University and Jang-Ting Guo of the University of California Riverside, summarized in my (1993) book *The Macroeconomics of Self-Fulfilling Prophecies*, we showed that the modern theory of rational expectations is fully consistent with the idea of confidence as a driving force of the business cycle.[4]

The idea that confidence can act as an independent shock to the economy was present in the work of classical economists like Pigou, but it was missing from the real business cycle model of Kydland and Prescott. In my work with Benhabib and Guo, we showed how to formalize this piece of classical theory that the rational expectations school missed using the same model as the real business cycle economists. We took the classical model of Pigou and provided a mathematical characterization of his ideas that allowed not only for productivity shocks, as in Kydland and Prescott's work, but also for shocks to confidence.

In my new book *Expectations, Employment and Prices* (2010), I have taken this idea much further. My most recent work bears the same relationship to the real business cycle model that Keynes's *General Theory* bears to the classical theory of Pigou. I have used the modern tools of rational expectations economics, not just to understand what Pigou meant by confidence, but also to understand what Keynes meant. All existing rational expectations theories assume that the natural rate hypothesis is true. I argue that it is false. As a consequence, I am able to explain how any long-run unemployment rate can persist forever. Confidence selects the unemployment rate that we observe.

My work provides an original explanation for why the Great Depression and the 2008 financial crisis occurred. The real business cycle model, the new-Keynesian model, and my own previous work with Benhabib and Guo all assume that the economy is self-stabilizing and that the unemployment rate is either equal to or close to the one that would be chosen by a social planner. None of these theories can explain the depth of human misery experienced during these events.

In contrast, the theory developed in *Expectations, Employment and Prices* explains how the unemployment rate can differ from its optimal rate for a very long time. My work *can* explain why depressions are so costly: And because I build on classical theory, rather than replacing it, my work is able to replicate all of the successes of classical ideas. Classical economics is the special case when confidence is high enough to maintain full employment.

BEHAVIORAL ECONOMICS OR RATIONAL CHOICE?

The idea that swings in confidence are rational is what distinguishes my research from behaviorist approaches that stress the role of psychology as a determinant of individual human behavior. Recent examples of applications of behaviorist approaches to economics include the popular books *Nudge*, by Thaler and Sunstein (2009), and *Animal Spirits*, by Akerlof and Shiller (2009), each of which draws conclusions using the idea that people are not fully rational and they need a little help sometimes.[5]

Unlike the behaviorists, I believe that individuals *are* rational. They know what is best for them, at least as well as anyone else, and they can make good guesses about the future that are right, on average. Behaviorists take the alternative view that what makes individuals truly happy can be different from what they in fact choose to do.[6] To a classical liberal like me, this is a scary proposition since it gives a license to someone else, someone who *does* know my true preferences, to act on my behalf. Is this the government or the church? Both institutions have claimed that right in the past with disturbing outcomes.

The rationality postulate in economics is often misunderstood. It is not a value judgment about right or wrong actions. It is a tautology. When economists say that homo economicus is rational, they mean only that human beings pursue goals to the best of their abilities. When Lucas (1972) extended this idea to talk about rational expectations, he meant only that individual human beings are not likely to be consistently mistaken. Rational expectations formalize the idea that you can't fool all of the people all of the time.

Keynes did not embrace rational expectations. But my goal is not to resuscitate failed interpretations of Keynes's *General Theory*. It is to build on his key ideas. Keynes never showed how his theory fits with classical economics. His followers assert that unemployment persists because wages and prices are slow to adjust to clear markets. But the money wage fell by 30% between 1929 and 1932. Unemployment does not persist because wages are inflexible. Unemployment persists because it is costly to match workers with jobs and there are no price signals to tell firms the best way to do this.

Before we get even further into debt as a society, it is important to understand why fiscal policy failed in the 1970s in a way that is consistent with evidence from the Great Depression. Appealing to behaviorist assumptions to justify Keynesian economics does not provide us with the explanation we seek. We need a new theory that integrates classical and Keynesian ideas.

In the monograph *Expectations, Employment and Prices*, I provide the science that backs up the claims in this chapter and in the other chapters of this book. In that monograph, I combine classical and Keynesian ideas in a way that explains the Great Depression of the 1930s, the stagflation of the 1970s, and the financial crisis of 2008 in a unified way. By looking at these events in a new light, I am able to suggest new remedies to prevent future crises from occurring and to help us out of the current one.

WEALTH MATTERS

The Great Depression occurred because firms could not sell enough goods to maintain full employment. Unemployed workers didn't have the purchasing power to buy goods, and that led to a vicious cycle that lasted for a decade. Keynes thought that aggregate demand depended mainly on income, but research on consumption in the 1950s proved that hypothesis to be incorrect. In fact, people spend more or less on goods and services based on wealth. Friedman (1957) showed that transitory fluctuations in income have a minor effect on consumption. What matters are sustained changes that he called permanent income, and other researchers identified with wealth. It follows that household wealth is a critical factor in determining the aggregate demand for goods and, in turn, the value of employment.[7] This fact has important consequences for the effectiveness of a fiscal stimulus.

During the 2008 crisis, everybody was affected. My colleagues at the University of California took a pay cut of anywhere from 4% to 10%, depending on their income, to help fill a California state budget gap of $26 billion. If this had occurred in 2004, faculty and staff would have borrowed against their housing equity to help finance college tuition bills, new automobile purchases, or vacations in Europe. But the value of real estate had dropped by 40% in some areas and retirement portfolios were devastated, causing even affluent families to cut back on their spending.

During the 1930s, many families owned tangible wealth in the form of bank accounts, but these assets disappeared as banks failed. Today, bank deposits are insured by the federal government, but direct ownership of risky assets in retirement accounts or direct ownership of stocks has become much more common. Wealth plays an important role in determining consumption, and when wealth falls and stays low for a protracted period of time, households are likely to cut back on their consumption, and aggregate demand for goods and services will fall.

WHERE KEYNESIAN ECONOMISTS WENT WRONG

Keynesian economists stress income as the main determinant of consumption. But although fluctuations in income are a factor in determining consumption, they are not the most important one. People recognize that fluctuations in income are often temporary. When income falls for six months because the breadwinner is between jobs, the household can often borrow against accumulated assets to maintain consumption. But when a person stays unemployed for a couple of years, his or her immediate sources of wealth quickly become exhausted.

It was a sustained drop in aggregate wealth that led to the depths and extent of unemployment at the time of the Great Depression, and it is a sustained drop in wealth that threatens to turn the 2008 crash into a very painful event. By stressing the role of income as a determinant of consumption, instead of wealth, Keynesian economists are led to advocate fiscal policy as the most effective remedy to restore full employment. I believe that they are wrong, and I am afraid that this mistake may be very costly since it will lead governments to accumulate large debts that our grandchildren will be asked to repay.

WHERE CLASSICAL ECONOMISTS WENT WRONG

According to modern versions of classical economics, the economy is driven by fundamentals: preferences, technology, and endowments. Since government regulation can affect the ability of firms to do business, changes in regulations, changes in taxes, or government interference in markets can also influence the fundamentals and, through that channel, cause a change in the number of people employed. But classical economics cannot account for a financial crisis or for a protracted depression of the kind we saw in the 1930s.

The U.S. economy has functioned pretty smoothly for the past 60 years, and although there have been 10 recessions since World War II, none of them has been nearly as severe as the Great Depression and most of them lasted for less than a year. The economy has been roughly four times less volatile since World War II than before the war, and economists began to think of the Great Depression as an anomaly that couldn't happen again. But in December 2007, the U.S. economy began to move into a deep recession that many contemporary observers compared with the onset of the Great Depression. By the fall of 2008, that recession had become worldwide in scope.

Many classical economists still see the economy as basically sound, and it is not uncommon to hear the government blamed as the source of all of our current problems. When the Fed chairman, Ben Bernanke, and the Treasury secretary, Henry Paulson, called on the government to provide $800 billion in emergency funding to help bail out troubled financial institutions, many economists cried foul and they blamed the crisis on the government itself; a colleague of mine asserted in a private conversation that "If only Bernanke and Paulson had left the banks to fail, the system would quickly have reestablished an equilibrium at full employment. Instead, Bernanke cried fire in a crowded theater and the response was predictable." Views similar to this have been voiced by many economists in recent days and are shared by a considerable number of academics, including some Nobel Prize winners.

I believe that the classical view is wrong for two reasons. First, modern classical economists ignore the role of confidence as an independent factor that drives booms and busts. Second, classical economists see the economy as a self-correcting mechanism in which market forces will restore full employment. They are wrong on both counts.

STOPPING A STAMPEDE

Although government actions such as the deregulation of the financial services industries have undoubtedly contributed to the current financial crisis, the view that the government is to blame for everything is surely overstated. The idea that government must be to blame follows logically from some versions of the classical theory, and those who defend this view are to be commended at least for consistency. But the crisis of 2008 was of a magnitude that had not previously been seen since the Great Depression. World stock markets fell by 20% in the first week of October 2008, and at that time the U.S. market was down 40% since its 2008 peak. According to classical economics, the markets were rationally anticipating a drop in future earnings, and since future earnings are determined by fundamentals, there must have been a collective knowledge of a very bad fundamental event that was just around the corner.

I fear that predictions of an imminent catastrophe for the real economy may well be correct. But the stock market is not an oracle that foresees an inevitable event that is triggered by fundamentals. In the 2008 presidential race, John McCain was criticized by Barack Obama for pronouncing that the "fundamentals of the economy are sound." Using the classical definition of fundamentals, McCain's view was correct in the sense that the economy had the same stock of factories and machines in 2009 that it had in 2008. But in the fall of 2008, the economy began hemorrhaging jobs at an alarming rate. What was the fundamental event foreseen by stock market participants that triggered this crisis?

In the classical theory of asset markets, fundamentals determine employment, employment determines profits, and profits determine the stock price. In the real world, confidence determines wealth, wealth determines demand, and demand determines employment. The only thing that keeps the economy on track is the collective confidence of hundreds of millions of investors that the economy is sound. But as experience has shown, investors are sometimes like buffalo grazing close to a cliff: Once a stampede starts in the wrong direction, it becomes a self-fulfilling prophecy that can be very hard to stop.

CHAPTER 9

Will There Be Another Great Depression?

Men who have created new fruits in the world cannot create a system whereby their fruits may be eaten. And the failure hangs over the State like a great sorrow. . . . [A]nd in the eyes of the people there is the failure; and in the eyes of the hungry there is a growing wrath. In the souls of the people the grapes of wrath are filling and growing heavy, growing heavy for the vintage.

—John Steinbeck (*The Grapes of Wrath*, 1939, chapter 25)

We often talk about the Great Depression as if it was a unique event, but similar episodes occurred in America and Europe in the nineteenth century and more recently great depressions have occurred in other countries around the world. Timothy Kehoe and Edward Prescott, two economists who have studied this issue, define a depression as a period of diminished economic activity with at least one year where output is 20% below the trend.[1] By this definition, Argentina, Brazil, Chile, and Mexico have all experienced great depressions since 1980. What are the chances that another great depression will occur in the United States?

TWO BLACK MONDAYS

The U.S. Great Depression began on Monday, October 28, 1929, when the stock market fell 13%, its second worst one-day decline in history. The worst was also on a Monday in October, but it did not occur for another 58 years. Both days have been described in the popular press as Black Monday.

To understand why many economists are worried that the 2008 Wall Street crash may have bad consequences for Main Street, take a look at Figure 9.1, which graphs the value of the S&P 500 and the unemployment rate for the early years of the Great Depression. The S&P 500 is the line marked by circles and is plotted on the left axis. The unemployment rate is the solid line plotted on the right axis. The unemployment rate is not available on a monthly

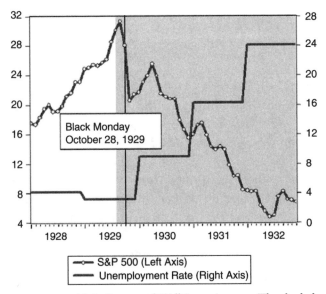

FIGURE 9.1 Main Street and Wall Street in 1929. The shaded region is an NBER recession.

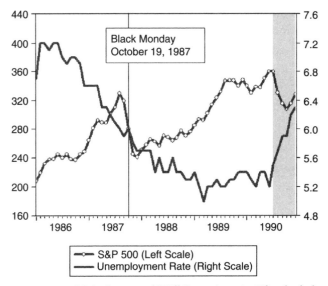

FIGURE 9.2 Main Street and Wall Street in 1987. The shaded region is an NBER recession.

basis for that period, which is why the unemployment series moves up in steps. Immediately following Black Monday in 1929, the U.S. unemployment rate began to climb from less than 8% in 1929 to 24% in 1932.

But although a big one-day decline in the stock market was followed by a depression in 1929, it is not true that big declines in the market are always followed by big declines in economic activity. On Monday, October 19,1987, the second and larger Black Monday in U.S. history, the S&P 500 dropped 21%, falling from 283 to 225 in one day, but this calamitous drop did not have much of an effect on employment. Why was 1987 different from 1929?

Figure 9.2 plots the S&P 500 and the unemployment rate for the period from 1986 through 1990. The S&P index is marked by circles and is measured on the left axis. The monthly unemployment rate is the solid line plotted on the right axis. This figure shows that although the market lost 21% of its value in one day, the decline did not last long and served only to wipe out gains that had built up over the previous year. Contrast this with the situation in 1929, where the S&P lost a third of its value in a month and continued to decline to 12% of its 1929 peak, a value that was lower in absolute terms than at any date since 1898.

GREENSPAN THE WIZARD

The fact that the market recovered relatively quickly in 1987 was due in part to the actions of the Fed. Alan Greenspan was aware of the history of the events of the 1930s and he responded to the huge drop in the stock market by announcing publicly that the Fed stood ready to lend any necessary amount of cash to the banks and to open a pipeline to the brokerage houses and investment banks that had lost money. On paper, U.S. investors had lost $500 billion in one day and most of the major U.S. financial institutions had become insolvent overnight with a greater value of outstanding liabilities than assets. The investment banks and brokerage houses were in desperate need of an injection of cash in order to settle short-term debts and remain afloat. The Fed recognized this need and announced that it would provide whatever liquidity was required.

The injection of credit by the Fed was successful: Asset values recovered and a second great depression did not materialize. By July 1989, the S&P 500 had regained its August 1987 peak and, as the market climbed, the financial assets of brokerage houses and investment banks were restored and U.S. financial institutions were able to repay the loans that had kept them solvent. An alternative outcome was always possible. If commercial banks had refused to lend to the brokerage houses and if major investment banks such as Goldman Sachs, Morgan Stanley, or Merrill Lynch had declared bankruptcy, the drop in the value of the market could well have become sustained and self-fulfilling. Then, as now, a great deal depends on the confidence of individual investors.

THE 2008 CRASH

In October 2008, the S&P 500 lost 40% of its value, and many commentators began to compare the situation to the Great Depression. The experience of the 1987 crash demonstrates that large drops in the value of the stock market are not always accompanied by depressions. So is 2008 more like 1930 or more like 1987? There are parallels with both situations. As in the 1930s, stock market wealth and the value of houses fell and unemployment began to climb. Unlike the 1930s, the Fed responded aggressively by lending money to the major financial institutions.

Consider first the behavior of unemployment and stock market wealth. Figure 9.3 plots the monthly values of the S&P and the unemployment rate from August 1998 to August 2008. The shaded regions represent the dates of the last two recessions, one of which began in March 2001 and ended in November of the same year, and the second of which began in December 2007.

It is clear from this figure that the value of stock market wealth fell dramatically from its peak in February 2007, and as of January 2008, it showed no sign of recovery. The fact that the economy entered a recession in December 2007 suggests that the drop in wealth had already begun to affect the real economy, and this fact alone suggests a closer parallel with the 1930s than with 1987. This is the first disturbing fact about the 2007 recession.

HOUSING AND STOCKS: TWIN PEAKS

A second disturbing fact is that housing prices were declining at the same time as a decline in the stock market. This fact makes the 2007 recession different from the 2001 recession, and according to a historical index of house prices constructed by Robert Shiller, the 2008 fall in nominal house prices was much bigger than the 10.5% drop in 1932, at the worst point of the Great Depression.[2]

Figure 9.3 shows not only the current recession but also the recession that lasted from March to November 2001. The 2001 recession occurred shortly after the end of a huge rise in the value of stocks that is popularly referred to as the "dot-com boom," because it was associated with the creation of companies based around information technology that had little or no current revenues but a small chance of

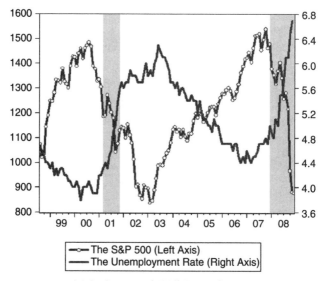

FIGURE 9.3 Main Street and Wall Street from 1998 to 2008. Shaded regions are NBER recessions.

very large potential future earnings. In 1999, the dot-com bubble collapsed and the value of stock market wealth began to decline.

The 2000 stock market collapse was different from the 2008 collapse because in 2000, stock market wealth was replaced by housing equity. At the same time that the stock market declined, the United States entered into a housing boom, and although U.S. households lost money from their stock portfolios, they gained from housing. It is likely that the housing boom helped households to maintain consumption, because as stock market wealth declined, housing wealth increased.

This point is illustrated graphically in Figure 9.4, which plots the S&P 500 and an index of housing prices, the Case-Shiller index, from August 1998 through December

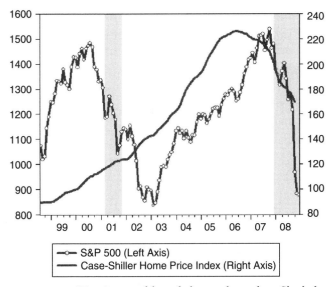

FIGURE 9.4 Housing wealth and the stock market. Shaded regions are NBER recessions.

2008. The Case-Shiller index is measured as the solid line and is plotted on the right axis. The S&P stock market index is measured as the line with circles and is plotted on the left axis. As the stock market began to decline in 2000, the value of house prices climbed to offset the fall in stocks.

DEREGULATION AND ACCOUNTING RULES

In the popular media, it has become common to blame the 2008 financial crisis on financial deregulation that occurred during the 1990s and on an accounting rule, "mark to market," that was introduced in the wake of the 1990s savings and loan crisis. Let's examine these arguments.

Before the Bank Act of 1933, commercial banks in the United States borrowed money from households in the form of bank deposits, and they lent money to other households to invest in houses and durable goods such as cars and refrigerators and to firms and small businesses, which used the money to finance their investment in factories and machines. These loans were illiquid, because although most loans will eventually be repaid, the bank could not ask for them to be repaid immediately.

Because banks made illiquid loans, they typically had much less cash on hand than they needed to meet their liabilities in the form of deposits. If all depositors were to try to withdraw their money immediately, there would not be enough cash to go around. For this reason, banks were often subject to panics. A rumor would spread that a bank had made risky investments and was insolvent, and this would cause all depositors to try to withdraw their money at once. For this reason, the house passed the Bank Act of 1933, sponsored by Senator Carter Glass and Congressman Henry B. Steagall.

THE END OF GLASS-STEAGALL

The Glass–Steagall Act created the Federal Deposit Insurance Corporation, which guaranteed bank deposits up to $100,000 (recently raised temporarily to $250,000), and it put a wall between commercial banks and investment banks by limiting the riskiness of the assets held by any bank that took direct deposits from the public. Before the Glass–Steagall Act, there were no restrictions on the kinds of loans that a bank could make. After the Glass–Steagall Act, banks were separated into two kinds: commercial banks and investment banks. Commercial banks were allowed to invest only in safe assets such as government bonds, and the depositors at these banks were insured by the federal government. Investment banks continued to make risky loans, but the owners of the liabilities of these banks were not insured against loss.

The argument for separating commercial and investment banks is that if the deposits of the bank are insured, then it has an incentive to make risky loans at high interest rates. If the loans perform well and are repaid, then the owners of the bank will make high profits. If the loans fail, then the depositors of the banks are protected by the government. Because depositors know that their savings are protected, they will be willing to place their money with the bank without risk and the taxpayers will be left to foot the bill if the loans turn sour.

Many of the provisions of the Glass–Steagall Act were repealed by the Gramm–Leach–Bliley Act of 1999. The Gramm–Leach–Bliley Act was followed by the movement of commercial banks into riskier high-return lending and was one of the main contributing factors to the trouble that now faces the financial services industry. Citibank and Bank of America were free to make riskier investments—and they did!

The repeal of the Glass-Steagall Act caused a reform of the banking industry that left all banks that took depositors' money free to invest that money anywhere. Throughout the United States, banks that had previously been purely commercial began to move into investment banking by purchasing riskier portfolios of assets including mortgage-backed securities. These securities were one of the main triggers of the financial meltdown that led to the collapse of Lehman Brothers in September 2008.

FAIR VALUE ACCOUNTING

A second regulatory change, introduced after the savings and loan crisis of the 1990s, was *fair value accounting*. Before its introduction, assets of financial institutions were typically valued at the price that the institution paid for them. This long-standing rule prevented market gyrations from spilling over into bank balance sheets and triggering insolvency. After the introduction of the new rules, banks and financial institutions were required to value assets at the price they could be sold for in the current market. This pricing rule is called "mark to market," and critics have blamed it for exacerbating the current financial crisis.[3] Defenders of mark-to-market argue that it introduces transparency and that it should be retained so that the shareholders of financial institutions are aware of what their shares are really worth.[4]

WAS DEREGULATION TO BLAME?

Deregulation has been widely criticized as the main cause of the 2008 financial crisis. Although it is certainly a contributing factor, I do not believe it is the main cause. There are two main criticisms of the regulatory changes that occurred in the 1990s. The first is that the repeal of the Glass-Steagall separation of commercial and investment banking led commercial banks to take unnecessary risks with depositors' funds. This overstates the case. The repeal of Glass-Steagall simply codified an implicit guarantee that had been there all along.

During the 1987 financial crisis, it was the investment banks that were in trouble—not the commercial banks—and at the time, the Glass-Steagall Act was still in place. Nevertheless, Alan Greenspan, implicitly or explicitly, channeled cash to the investment banks to prevent their collapse. Were these banks undergoing a temporary liquidity crisis or were they insolvent? The answer to this question is important but by no means obvious, and it is a question to which classical and Keynesian economics give different answers.

ILLIQUIDITY OR INSOLVENCY?

Is the banking sector insolvent? If the classical economists are right, then the answer to this question does not depend on the actions of the Fed. In 1987, the investment banks were either insolvent or they were not. If the stock market crash had been caused by investors correctly anticipating that future fundamentals were bad, then the banks were insolvent and Greenspan, by bailing them out, was wasting taxpayers' money. The fact that the bailout was successful implies, according to this view, that Greenspan knew more than the markets. He is indeed a wizard, and he was able to correctly forecast that the fundamentals of the economy were in fact sound.

If Keynesian economics is right, there was a real danger in 1987 that the drop in the market would turn out to be self-fulfilling. By pumping liquidity into the system, Greenspan convinced investors to regain confidence in stocks and his actions rescued the economy from a second great depression that could have occurred but was not inevitable. This was a gamble that paid off then, but it is not guaranteed always to have the same outcome. If the actions of the Fed had not restored confidence, the Fed would have lost a lot of taxpayer money and a depression would have occurred in spite of its actions.

WHAT WILL HAPPEN NEXT?

Is the 2008 situation more like 1929 or more like 1987? There are parallels with both cases. Like 1987, the Fed stepped in to provide liquidity to the markets. But as of July 2009, the markets had not been noticeably calmed. For most of the postwar period, house prices had gone up and housing was widely viewed as a relatively safe investment. The strong performance of the housing market led to the creation of mortgage-backed securities, which are assets whose payments of principal and interest derive from cash flows generated by mortgages. This market was nonexistent in 1970 but had grown to $7.5 trillion by the end of 2007, of which roughly $6 trillion was issued by the semiautonomous bodies Ginnie Mae and Freddie Mac and implicitly guaranteed by the U.S. government.[5] It is the portion of the mortgage-backed-securities market that is not guaranteed that triggered the financial crisis of 2008.

When U.S. house prices began to fall in 2007, the default rates on mortgage-backed securities turned out to be higher than anyone had predicted, and financial institutions throughout the world discovered that they were holding assets that were potentially worth much less than their book value. But what were they really worth? This question began as one of confidence in the U.S. economy and it spread—in January 2009—to one of the confidence of investors worldwide. Factories, machines, and houses, worldwide, are worth what investors will pay for them. If these assets remain undervalued, then default rates on mortgages in the United States and elsewhere will be high and a catastrophic drop in property values will be self-fulfilling. As wealth drops, demand will fall and workers will lose their jobs all over the world. It would be a grave mistake to think that a worldwide depression of this kind cannot happen again. It would be an equally grave mistake to assume that a depression, if it occurs, is inevitable and is caused purely by fundamentals that are beyond our control. But is there anything that government can or should do about the situation? I will take up that question in the following chapters.

CHAPTER 10

Will Monetary and Fiscal Policy Work?

It may seem very wise to sit back and wag the head. But while we wait, the unused labour of the workless is not piling up to our credit in a bank, ready to be used at some later date. It is running irrevocably to waste; it is irretrievably lost. Every puff of Mr. Baldwin's pipe costs us thousands of pounds.

—John Maynard Keynes (1931, p. 120 of the 1963 Norton edition)

In America, the 1920s was a time of prosperity. But Great Britain entered a depression in the early 1920s and remained there for 20 years. There were already 2 million unemployed by 1930. Keynes wrote the words in this opening quote in 1929 to urge more active government policy than that which had been pursued by Stanley Baldwin, the conservative prime minister of England from 1924 through 1929. Prime Minister Baldwin didn't listen to him. With the benefit of hindsight, President Obama, Prime Minister Gordon Brown, and President Nicolas Sarkozy did.

Since 1936, when Keynes wrote *The General Theory*, policymakers have used two tools, monetary and fiscal policy, to combat recessions. Monetary policy works by lowering the interest rate. This makes it more attractive for private companies to invest in real assets such as factories, machines, and houses and it increases aggregate demand indirectly by raising expenditure by the private sector.

Fiscal policy is more direct but acts more slowly. It works by increasing the demand for goods as government borrows to build roads and bridges or by cutting taxes and putting more spending power in the hands of households. Monetary and fiscal policy are both designed to increase aggregate demand and thereby to cause firms to employ more workers. This chapter explains these policies and outlines the options available to central banks and national treasuries to combat financial crises.

TRADITIONAL MONETARY POLICY

Although the government can combat recessions with monetary or fiscal policy, monetary policy is the tool of choice. It works by stimulating private spending and is faster acting than fiscal policy.

When the economy moves into recession, the central bank lowers the yield on safe assets. In the United States, this works through Fed purchases of Treasury bills on the open market. In the UK and in Europe, the mechanism is a little different but the effect is the same. The central bank lowers the interest rate to stimulate the economy in a recession by injecting liquidity into the financial system. As commercial banks try to lend the additional money, interest rates fall and more risky business ventures become profitable. As firms and households begin to purchase more goods, this increases employment and helps to bring the economy out of recession. This strategy has worked in all of the last 10 postwar recessions, but it is not available to the Fed, the European Central Bank, or the Bank of England today.

There have been 10 complete recessions in the United States since the end of World War II and in every one of them the Fed helped the economy out of a recession by lowering the Fed funds rate. But today, just as in 1934, the interest rate on Treasuries is close to zero, and traditional monetary policy can't go any further. If the Fed buys Treasury bills and replaces them with cash, it is replacing one zero interest rate government liability with another. This is a little like exchanging a 10-dollar bill for two fives. When the interest rate on Treasury bills is zero, money and bonds become perfect substitutes and the traditional method of running open market operations is like "pushing on a string".[1]

QUANTITATIVE EASING

Since the scope for traditional monetary policy is limited, the Fed and the Bank of England are following a new approach: *quantitative easing*. The European Central Bank is following a similar strategy, and all three are injecting money into the system in an effort to bring down interest rates on risky assets and long-term government debt. Traditionally, the Fed has conducted open market operations by buying and selling three-month Treasury bills. Quantitative easing refers to an alternative monetary policy of expanding the money supply by buying a range of alternative assets including corporate debt and long-term government bonds.

In August 2008, the Fed owned assets of approximately $800 billion, most of it in the form of three-month Treasury bills. By January 2009, that figure had more than doubled as the Fed made short-term loans to the financial sector and began direct interventions in the commercial paper market. Commercial paper is an unsecured loan with a duration of less than nine months, and in normal times these loans are issued by commercial banks to nonfinancial corporations that use the funds to meet payroll and short-term obligations.

Since November 2008, the Fed has begun to buy commercial paper and has replaced commercial banks as the main lender in this market. By directly lending in the commercial paper market, the Fed is engaging in quantitative easing. Chairman Bernanke has indicated that we are likely to see much more of this in the future, and the Bank of England's monetary policy committee is committed to a similar approach.

BERNANKE'S PLAN

Some idea of Chairman Bernanke's intentions can be gleaned from a speech he gave to the Japan Society of Monetary Economics in Tokyo, Japan (May 31, 2003). In that speech, he laid out a plan to aid Japanese recovery that he is now following to combat the recession in the United States.

Bernanke pointed out that although the interest rate on short-term securities may be close to zero, it is still possible for the nation's central bank to purchase other kinds of assets. One example is the purchase of long-term government bonds. This policy would work in exactly the same way as traditional monetary policy, but instead of buying three-month Treasury bills—for which the interest rate is already at zero—the Fed would buy longer-term government bonds. As of January 2009, long-term government bonds were yielding a return of between 1.5% and 2.0% depending on the maturity. The hope was that, as government drives down the return on long-term bonds, households will put their money back into the stock market, and U.S. corporations will be encouraged to invest in new plants and equipment.

In his 2003 address in Japan, Chairman Bernanke laid out a program by which the Treasury and the Fed would cooperate to coordinate monetary and fiscal policy. If his proposal were to be applied to the U.S. situation, it would involve the following steps. First, the Treasury would announce a large fiscal stimulus to be paid for by printing money. Second, the Fed would announce an explicit target for the inflation rate. The purpose of this announcement is to anchor the expectations of the public by giving them a clear guide to Fed intentions in future months if inflation begins to reappear. Third, the Fed would engage in a program of quantitative easing by buying a range of assets other than the traditional Fed purchases of three-month Treasury bills.

As of January 2009, the Obama administration had announced plans for an $800 billion increase in the federal deficit and, if Bernanke were to follow step one of the strategy outlined in his advice to the Japanese, the Fed would finance the Obama plan by printing money. Under step two of the plan, as the economy began to expand, the Fed would sell government securities on the open market to absorb the excess liquidity that it created in step one. This would prevent the money supply from expanding too quickly and generating inflation. Step three of the Bernanke plan— quantitative easing—would involve the purchase of a range of alternative private and government securities including corporate paper and long-term bonds issued by government and private corporations.

How would the Bernanke plan work? The following section explains what the Fed, the Bank of England, and the European Central Bank believe and why, in the view of central bankers, a plan like this makes sense.

WHAT CENTRAL BANKERS THINK

Central bank policymakers throughout the world believe there is a natural rate of unemployment that the economy moves toward in the long run and they believe that monetary and fiscal policy cannot influence this natural rate. In the short run, however, they believe that the unemployment rate may move away from its natural rate because of shocks to demand and supply. An example of a supply shock is a big unexpected increase in the price of oil, such as occurred in 1973 and again in 1979. An example of a demand shock is a big unexpected drop in house prices of the kind we saw in 2007.

Policymakers I have spoken with at the Fed believe, and I think they are right, that the 2007 financial crisis was generated by a demand shock as households revised downward their estimates of the future profitability of real estate investments. Market participants came to the collective realization that previous house price growth was unsustainable, and since houses in the United States are two-fifths of household wealth and in the UK they are closer to three-fifths of wealth, this realization led to a big drop in aggregate demand. As demand fell, firms laid off workers and the house price fall was translated into lost jobs in the real economy. The drop in employment caused a further loss in confidence, which caused investors to sell stocks and shares and to buy Treasury bills instead. This led to a 40% fall in world stock markets caused by a fear that profits would fall and that many companies may become insolvent.

WHEN THE BUBBLE BURSTS

When asset price increases are unjustified by underlying fundamentals, economists call this a bubble. For example, a person may buy a second house, expecting to sell it quickly at a higher price, even though the rents that can be earned on the house are not large enough to justify the price that was paid.

In a bubble, the price of an asset keeps going up and people are prepared to buy it because they expect future price increases. These increases are ultimately unsustainable, and eventually the bubble bursts. It seems likely that the recent crash was triggered by a bursting bubble in the U.S. housing market. But why did this cause an increase in unemployment?

The consensus central bank position is that demand shocks, such as a bursting bubble, can affect real activity only to the extent that prices are slow to adjust. It follows that there will need to be a period of price adjustment as house prices fall to a new lower, sustainable level. That adjustment process will likely require money wages and the prices of many other commodities to fall, too. Because wages and prices cannot fall fast enough, unemployment will increase in the short term.

From the central bank perspective, there is an alternative preferable scenario to a protracted period of falling prices. It is to flood the economy with money so that prices and wages do not have to fall. Monetary policy stimulates demand by lowering interest rates, but this cannot work today, because the interest rate is already at zero. Quantitative easing involves trying to bring down the spreads on risky assets by lending directly to firms or by bringing down the premium on long bonds by directly purchasing long-term government debt. This might work, but there is no guarantee that it will cause firms to invest in new factories and machines. Instead, we might end up in a situation where corporate paper and long bonds pay a zero interest rate and the Fed absorbs any associated default risk.

OBAMA, BROWN, AND SARKOZY

As of January 2009, the Obama administration was proposing a fiscal stimulus of the order of $800 billion, spread over two years, of which two-thirds would be increased government expenditure and one-third would be in the form of tax cuts. In the UK, Gordon Brown's fiscal deficits were projected to be even larger as a percentage of UK GDP, and in Europe, politicians were divided, with different policies being followed in every different country.

The U.S. fiscal expansion is of the order of 5% of GDP, and it will likely take the federal budget deficit above 10% of GDP. To put the numbers into perspective, it is roughly $2,700 for every man, woman, and child in the United States. The debate over how to spend this money is intense.

If the only concern were to get the economy back on track, then the fastest way to get things moving would be to send a check for $2,700 to every U.S. resident. If the administration were worried about the distribution of income, this check could be counted as taxable income, thereby requiring high earners to pay some of it back. A family of four would receive $10,800, and it is likely that much of that money would be spent immediately on goods and services. This way of increasing aggregate demand would be immediate, and it could be as large as needed. It has the advantage that the money would stay in the hands of households and would not create large new government programs. Would it work? Administration economists think so.

CHRISTINA ROMER'S MAGIC MULTIPLIER . . . IS IT REALLY THAT BIG?

Christina Romer, chair of the Council of Economic Advisors, is a leading academic with a substantial body of research to back up her views. Her research has led her to the opinion that the effects of a tax cut could be substantial.

> We [David Romer and I] found that the estimated effect of these changes is very large. A tax cut of 1% of GDP raises GDP by between 2 and 3% over the next three years.[2]

Although Christina Romer thinks the multiplier could be as large as 3, other economists are more cautious. A consensus view is that a $1 increase in government expenditure will cause an increase in GDP of as much as $1.5. The ratio of the increase in GDP to the increase in expenditure is called the multiplier, and the theory behind it is based on Keynesian economics.[3]

The dramatic differences in estimates of the size of the multiplier arise because there is little reliable empirical evidence. In the real world, everything is changing at once, and when GDP goes up it's difficult to tell whether the cause was an increase in government spending or something else. Economists are unable to conduct controlled experiments on the economy. If we could increase government expenditure and hold everything else constant, we might be able to isolate the effect of an expenditure increase on GDP. This is what a scientist would do in a laboratory to test a theory. Instead, we must rely on nature or politicians to experiment for us.

As of July 2009, a third of the U.S. stimulus was slated to be spent as tax cuts. Since the money would be directed at low-income households that do not pay taxes, these "cuts" are actually transfers from government to households. In addition to tax cuts, the U.S. plan contained provisions to help the states: These included a $79 billion state stabilization fund and an $87 billion increase in federal support for Medicaid. Since many U.S. states are prevented from borrowing to finance deficits by state constitutions, both of these portions of the bill will help to prevent job cuts that would otherwise occur at the state level. The remaining portions of the bill are directed at infrastructure investment, health, education, and energy, and critics have pointed out, that although these expenditures will help support long-term growth, they may act too slowly to have an immediate impact on the 2008–2009 recession.

The UK and France enacted similar fiscal stimulus plans, and many other economies followed suit. The motivation behind these expenditure increases was Keynesian. In the United States, administration economists have argued that an increase in government purchases will cause consumption to increase and that the cumulative effect of increased government purchases and increased private expenditure will be large enough to restore full employment. What can we learn from history about the likely success of these stimulus plans?

LEARNING FROM THE GREAT DEPRESSION

The next best thing to holding everything constant is to make a very large change in a variable of interest and see what happens to everything else. For example, if we observe an unusually large increase in government expenditure, then we can infer that unusual simultaneous changes in employment, consumption, or GDP were probably caused by the change in government purchases.

Large dramatic increases in the size of government don't occur often. Even during the Great Depression, the increase in government in the United States was gradual and the really dramatic changes did not occur until World War II. At that time, however, we did see a remarkable and unusual change as government purchases on goods and services increased from 12% of GDP in 1940 to 50% in 1944: It was the wartime stimulus that pulled the United States out of the Great Depression, not Roosevelt's New Deal, as some commentators have claimed.

THE FIRST STAGE OF RECOVERY

U.S. GDP at the depth of the Great Depression was 25% below trend. The economy recovered in two stages. Stage 1 of the recovery lasted from 1933 to 1937, and during this stage, GDP increased by 12.5%. Between May 1937 and June 1938, there was a recession. Stage 2 of the recovery

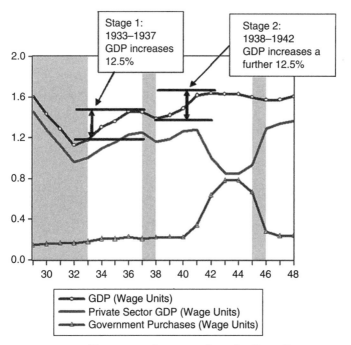

FIGURE 10.1 Two stages of recovery from the Great Depression. Shaded regions are NBER recessions.

was from 1938 to 1942, and during this second stage, GDP increased by a further 12.5% to bring the economy back to full capacity. How much of this recovery was due to fiscal policy?

Figure 10.1 breaks GDP into private and public components for the period from 1929 through 1948. The bottom line marked by triangles measures government purchases; the solid line in the middle is the private sector component of GDP; and the top line, marked by circles, is the sum of the other two parts: This represents the real value of all goods and services produced in the United States in a given year.[4]

A couple of things stand out on this figure. First, in stage 1 of the recovery from the Great Depression, between 1933 and 1937, the real value of government expenditures was tiny. Observe the lower line in Figure 10.1, which looks flat between 1933 and 1937. The size of Roosevelt's stimulus was negligible compared with the later wartime expansion and the increase in government purchases over this period looks a lot more like a slowly moving gentle trend than a Keynesian fiscal experiment.

THE SECOND STAGE OF RECOVERY

Second, in stage 2 of the recovery, from 1938 to 1942, the increase in the size of government was truly massive. In Figure 10.1, this shows up as the upward blip in government purchases (the lower line in the figure) during World War II. Large movements of this kind are rare in economic time series, but they are incredibly valuable because large unpredicted movements are natural experiments. We can use this experiment to ask: How large was the multiplier during World War II?

My calculations using evidence from this period indicate that when there is high unemployment, the multiplier is close to 1 not 1.5 or larger, as some have suggested. When we are at full employment, the multiplier is equal to zero. In other words, if there is excess capacity in the economy, then for every dollar of extra expenditure by government, GDP will increase by $1. Once we reach capacity, every dollar of extra expenditure by government will result in no change in GDP; instead, it will crowd out $1 of private expenditure.

To sum up, the data from World War II suggest that, in the current economic climate, an $800 billion increase in government purchases in the United States is likely to lead to an $800 billion increase in GDP, or at best two-thirds of the increase that the administration is projecting since their calculations are based on the assumption that the multiplier is 1.5. Although the proposed Obama stimulus package will create jobs, it is unlikely that they will be created in the private sector, and it seems that we may be headed for the largest increase in the size of government since World War II.

TWO REASONS FOR GOVERNMENT DEFICITS

There are two reasons for running budget deficits. The first is that unemployment is too high and social resources are being wasted. The second is to fund projects that government can provide more effectively than the private sector. These two reasons are being confounded in the current debate, and I am concerned that the possibility of the world entering a second Great Depression is being used, at least in the United States, as a tactic to rush new spending programs into law without proper debate.

Economists are divided as to the likely effectiveness of the current stimulus. I have two concerns. One is similar to the criticisms raised by many conservative politicians. The second is more fundamental. Let me deal first with the conservative position.

DO WE NEED A BIGGER GOVERNMENT?

There are good arguments for the social provision of health insurance, for the creation of a smart electric grid, for fixing roads and bridges, and for new public transportation projects. But there are costs to all of these expenditures, each of which involves an expansion of the government sector at the cost of the private sector. It is disingenuous to argue that these components of the plan should be passed as swiftly as possible on the grounds that a second Great Depression can only be prevented by a massive increase in the size of government.

The best way to swiftly enact a fiscal stimulus is to print money and hand out checks to every taxpayer. A rebate of $2,700 per household seems like a good place to start in the U.S. case. As the economy begins to recover, the Fed should remove the excess liquidity from the system through an announced policy of raising the interest rate to meet an inflation target of 2%. This would help to reduce the threat that the stimulus will create inflation. The expenditure component of the Obama proposal, in my view, requires more considered debate and should be treated for what it is: a long-term investment in America's future.

As with any long-term investment, the creation of new social infrastructure will create productive capital. If this investment is carefully chosen, it will promote growth and generate future benefits that pay for themselves through increased tax revenues.

A new electric grid may allow firms to produce goods more efficiently. An improved rail network may reduce the costs of transportation and increase productivity. If this is the case, then increased productivity will result in higher wages and higher profits that will swell the coffers of government through increased tax revenues. If this is not the case, then investments of this kind should not be considered.

Not all infrastructure projects are worthwhile. The Alaska bridge to nowhere that was a focus of the recent political campaign is a case in point, and it is because some social investments are ill considered that national legislatures should carefully weigh the costs and benefits of each project before committing taxpayer money to possible wasteful spending.

WILL THE STIMULUS RESTORE CONFIDENCE?

The concerns I have addressed previously are likely to be shared by many other economists. I have a second, more fundamental concern that follows from the unique perspective that I have put forward in this book. Unlike classical and new-Keynesian economists, I do not hold the view that there is a unique natural rate of unemployment that is independent of aggregate demand. The success of any given stimulus plan will depend as much on building confidence of the private sector as it does on increasing aggregate demand, because not all increases in aggregate demand are translated into increased jobs.

GIVE ME A ONE-ARMED ECONOMIST

Economists are famous for hedging their bets. A typical response to the question of how to run fiscal policy might be: "On the one hand, we should raise taxes, but on the other, we should balance the budget." President Harry Truman, who instituted the Council of Economic Advisors famously quipped, "Give me a one-armed economist." In this spirit, here is my answer to the question: Are we enacting the right policies?

Here are my views on fiscal policy. A large fiscal stimulus may or may not be an important component of a recovery plan. I believe there is a better alternative to fiscal policy, which I explain in chapter 11. But if a fiscal policy *is* used, it should take the form of transfer payment to every domestic resident, not an increase in government expenditure.

Here are my views on monetary policy. Short-term interest rates should be increased as soon as feasible, because a positive interest rate is needed if a national central bank is to effectively control inflation. In the future, central banks should use the interest rate for this purpose and not to prevent recessions.

But if a central bank raises the domestic interest rate without independently managing confidence, the result will be a drop in the value of the national stock market and a further deterioration in the real economy. To prevent this from happening, central banks need a second instrument. The following chapter explains what this instrument is and how to use it. I propose a strategy for managing confidence that will put an end to the cycle of boom and bust that has characterized capitalist economies for the past 300 years.

CHAPTER 11

How to Solve a Financial Crisis

He that will not apply new remedies must expect new evils; for time is
the greatest innovator.

—Francis Bacon (*Essays*, "Of Great Place")

The history of world economies since World War II has been one of recurrent alternating periods of booms and recessions. In the United States there were 10, four to five-year expansions during which unemployment fell and GDP grew, followed by short, sharp contractions during which unemployment rose by an average of 3.5%. Although international business cycles are not perfectly correlated, the continental European and UK experiences have been similar to those of the United States.

In each case and in each country where they occurred, contractions did not end on their own; they all had a little help. In the United States, the Fed lowered interest rates in every postwar recession. The Great Depression was different precisely because this option was not available. By 1934, the fed funds rate, call rates, and overnight loan rates were effectively zero.

According to real business cycle theory—the dominant economic theory that we have been teaching in our finest academic institutions for 35 years—the wage adjusts quickly to ensure that employment is determined by the equality of the demand and supply of labor: Anyone without a job in a financial crisis is simply asking for too much money and the unemployment rate is the one that would be chosen by a benevolent social planner.

I do not deny that productivity shocks can have effects on GDP; but Pigou (1929) listed six causes of business cycles, and the other five are also important factors. A war in the Persian Gulf that cuts the world oil supply in half would surely cause a recession in countries that import oil. But not all of the shocks to the world price of oil are obviously caused by changes in fundamentals: Market psychology is just as important.

Market psychology takes small fundamental shocks and amplifies them through panic in the financial markets. In the classical world, a single cool-headed investor could bet against the market and help to steer the economy back toward full employment. Such a far-sighted investor would make considerable profit in the process. The reason that no such investor emerged in the 2008 financial crisis is that there *is* no unique definition of full employment. The invisible hand has palsy.

WHAT HAPPENED IN 2008

In the 2008 crisis, the world economy was headed rapidly toward a high-unemployment, low-wealth equilibrium triggered by a loss of confidence in the value of assets, backed by mortgages in the U.S. subprime mortgage market. The inability to value these assets led to an amplification of the crisis as panic hit the global financial markets.

The U.S. stock market was appropriately valued in early 2009, based on historical price earnings ratios. But investors were worried that the value of stocks could fall further. In the summer of 2008, the Dow Jones index of industrial stocks was trading at around 12,000. In February 2009, it was down at 8,000. If the Dow were to fall further, the drop would be self-fulfilling and both financial and nonfinancial institutions throughout the world would continue to become insolvent in record numbers.

It is widely believed by economists and financial journalists that we were in a liquidity crisis in 2008. The talk in Washington, Frankfurt, Tokyo, and London was that we must unfreeze the credit markets, and many observers expressed puzzlement that investment banks and other financial institutions were holding onto capital, newly acquired from national central banks, and were refusing to lend it to corporations. But in fact, the strategy of holding onto cash was rational for each bank individually.

Banks in 2009 were concerned that the market had further to fall. If the values of houses, factories, and machines were to continue to fall, loans to corporations would not be repaid and the banks would lose money. As of February 2009, the market was in a holding pattern in which market participants were terrified that things could get much worse.

ADDING A NEW POLICY LEVER

Since 1951, the Fed has reacted to recessions by lowering the interest rate. Although central banks have been largely successful at preventing a major depression from reoccurring, at least until now, policymakers have misunderstood the nature of the game that they are engaged in. Policymakers at national central banks believe they can influence the domestic inflation rate in the long run but that central bank policy has no influence on the domestic long-run unemployment rate. Although it is surely correct that monetary policy can influence inflation in the long run, the central thesis of this book is that the central bank can also have a permanent effect on unemployment.

A nation's central bank controls two levers of economic policy. The first is the size of its balance sheet, which determines the stock of money circulating in the economy. The second is the composition of its balance sheet. Until recently, central banks have almost exclusively held reserves in the form of gold or more recently as loans to national governments. With the advent of inflation targeting in the 1980s, central bankers learned to use the first lever to control inflation, but only now are they experimenting with the second. It's a bit like learning how to turn the rudder of a sailboat without knowing how to raise or lower the sails.

In November 2008, the Fed and the Bank of England began to purchase different kinds of assets in a policy of quantitative easing. This was the right approach, but it didn't go far enough. It is time for an expanded role for direct policy intervention in the asset markets through a policy that targets not just one price, the short-term interest rate, but two. In addition to using the size of their balance sheets to change the interest rate and target inflation, policymakers should use the composition of central bank balance sheets to change asset prices and target the unemployment rate. This need not involve the direct purchase of voting shares in individual companies. A better plan would be to trade a stock market index fund.

INDICES AND INDEX FUNDS

A stock market index is a weighted sum of the prices of a given basket of stocks. There are many such indices that differ in the composition of the firms in the basket and the importance given to individual stocks. Some indices give equal weight to every firm in the index. Others give larger firms more weight. Examples of well-known indices include the Dow Jones Industrial, the Standard and Poor's 500, and the Wilshire 5000 in the United States, the FTSE 100 in the UK; and the Nikkei in Japan. By construction, a stock market index is defined equal to 100 at its inception by appropriately choosing the weights of each individual stock.

For example, suppose that we were to define a new index, the Farmer Big 3, that consisted of three stocks: Wal-Mart, Microsoft, and Apple. As of February 10, 2009, these were trading at $47.8, $19.17, and $98.74 a share, respectively. The value of a company can be defined as the price of its shares multiplied by the number of shares outstanding. This is called the market capitalization of the firm, and as of February 10, 2009, the market capitalization of the Farmer Big 3 was $187 billion for Wal-Mart, $170 billion for Microsoft, and $88 billion for Apple. The total value of the three companies was $445 billion, of which 42% was Wal-Mart, 38% was Microsoft, and 20% was Apple. These figures are summarized in table 11.1.

The Farmer Big 3 was initiated on February 10, 2009, so its value, by definition, was 100 on that day. Now suppose that on February 11 Wal-Mart and Microsoft continue to

TABLE 11.1   The Farmer Big 3 Index

	Wall Mart		Microsoft		Apple	
	Price	Mkt. Cap	Price	Mkt. Cap	Price	Mkt. Cap
Weight	$47.8	$187b 42%	$19.17	$170b 38%	$98.74	$88b 20%

trade at $47.8 and $19.17, but the price of Apple falls by half and it trades that day at $49.37. Wal-Mart and Microsoft are unchanged, but Apple has dropped by 50%. Since Apple makes up only 20% of the index, the Farmer Big 3 will drop by 50% times 20%, for a fall of 10%, and its value on February 11 will be 90.

Stock market indices are barometers of the market. They tell us how an average of stocks is performing.

Not all investors have the time or the inclination to keep up with market trends and to actively trade a portfolio of stocks. Mutual funds are ways to pay someone else to manage your stock portfolio for you. Until recently, all mutual funds were actively managed by a financial professional who decided on the composition of the portfolio from day to day.

In 1975, John Bogle, the founder of Vanguard, introduced a completely new idea into the market: an index fund. This is a mutual fund that holds a portfolio of stocks in proportion to the fixed weights of an index and issues liabilities that are held by savers, backed by the underlying stocks. The first fund started by Vanguard began with assets of $11 million, and by 1999, it had more than $100 billion.

A PLAN TO PREVENT BUBBLES AND CRASHES

Individual stocks rise and fall as the fundamentals of the economy change. A new oil field will increase the value of the company that discovers it. A successful North Korean missile test will boost stocks of defense contractors. The discovery of a new vaccine will raise the fortunes of its manufacturer. Some fundamental events move all stocks at the same time. If a government is elected on the platform of raising business taxes, all stock prices will fall, because the after-tax value of dividends will be lower.

Fundamentals are not the only factors that move markets. Individual stocks rise and fall because of changes in market psychology that may be difficult to disentangle from true fundamental events. How will nanotechnology alter the profits of companies five years from now? How will the Internet affect business in 10 years' time? Will computers ever be more intelligent than humans? These are all examples of events that could have profound effects on the value of future dividends, but their effects are very difficult to quantify.

Because the value of wealth is closely linked to the value of demand, and thereby to employment, vague beliefs about future dividends can become self-fulfilling. By stabilizing large market movements, both up and down, the central bank can prevent these movements from adversely affecting the real economy. Control of an index fund is the ideal way to implement this idea, because it would not require a national central bank to directly own stock in private corporations.

SETTING UP A FUND

To implement this plan, one first needs to define an index. Since it is all of domestic wealth that is the target, the index should include all publicly traded companies. To prevent small companies from having a big influence on policy, these companies would need to be weighted in some way. Companies with large market capitalization or companies with large numbers of employees should have high weight in the index. Some kind of rule would need to be put in place that allows the weights to be changed periodically as companies grow or shrink and new companies are created.

Once the index is defined, private investment companies such as Vanguard or Fidelity would be encouraged to create index funds based on the announced weights for market stock. These companies would buy shares in the private companies and hold them as assets. They would create offsetting liabilities in the form of index funds and sell them on the market.

Once a market is established in the newly defined index funds, the central bank would purchase an initial block of index funds at the market price. In the U.S. case, the balance sheet of the Fed at the end of 2008 was about $800 billion, and a similar number for index funds might be a good starting place. An important part of this plan is that intervention by the central bank in the stock market should be independent of its control of the money supply. To achieve this independence, the bank would issue three-month interest-bearing bonds, guaranteed by the national treasury.

PULLING THE LEVER

When a central bank sets the interest rate, this is typically announced for a one-to two-month period. The Open Market Committee of the Fed meets eight times a year, and at each meeting it has traditionally announced the interest rate on Fed funds for the next six weeks. To maintain this interest rate, it intervenes in the market by buying and selling Treasury bills in exchange for money. An expanded Fed would announce, at the same time, a price path for index funds, and it would stand ready to buy and sell these funds each day at the announced price. More generally, a domestic central bank might announce that it will begin trading a newly created index fund one week from the date of its meeting at a price of 120 and that the price will be adjusted daily to grow at an annual rate of 3%. If the current value of the index were 100, then fund managers would have an incentive to buy blocks of shares in the underlying companies until the value of the fund were bid up to the announced value at which the central bank will trade.

Wouldn't the taxpayer lose money? That event is extremely unlikely. Central banks earn interest on their assets and traditionally they have not paid interest on their liabilities. The interest earned is typically used to pay for operating expenses, and anything left over is returned to the national treasury. The operation of stock market stabilization would pay a return equal to the dividends of the companies held in the index fund. This would represent a net flow into the central bank each month. It would cost the central bank to operate a plan like this since it would pay interest on the securities issued to buy the index fund. For the scheme to break even, the inflows must balance the outflows.

Historically, the U.S. stock market has earned a premium of around 5% over Treasury bills. This premium is poorly understood, but economists think that it is due to the risk of holding stocks—particularly the kind of systemic risk that we witnessed with the 2008 crash. Since the market stabilization plan that I propose would remove this systemic risk, it is unlikely that the stock market would continue to earn a large premium over treasuries. It is more likely that the return to the market would fall, and the interest rate on Treasury bills would rise. Since the central bank would be purchasing the index fund at a time when market values are very low, it is likely that—over the long term—the scheme would more than pay for itself.

HOW TO FIX THE BANKS

The idea of using an index fund to support asset prices has other potential applications. A more limited version of this same idea provides a way for a central bank to inject new equity into its national banking sector without owning the banks or nationalizing them. How would this work?

The plan is a simple extension of control of a market index in which the central bank buys and sells a limited index of bank stocks rather than the entire market. It would involve the following four steps.

First, define an indexed fund that would include all publicly traded bank stocks with weights based on initial market capitalization and a rule that allows the weights to be adjusted periodically.

Second, allow private financial corporations to create and trade this fund by purchasing bank shares as assets and selling the indexed fund as a liability.

Third, direct the central bank to purchase an initial block of index funds and pay for it by issuing newly created short-term interest-bearing debt backed by the Treasury but issued by the central bank.

Fourth, at each meeting of the national monetary policy committee, announce a price, and a rate of growth for this price, at which the central bank would be willing to buy and sell the index fund over the next few weeks.

Banks were undervalued in January 2009 because there was no market for the "toxic assets" that they held. How would the central bank decide on the correct value of these assets? Under the scheme I have suggested here, it wouldn't have to. The market would decide what they're worth. The relative price of each bank stock would be determined by marketplace trades and not by the central bank. As new information came in about the underlying values of a bank's assets, the bank's value would rise or fall.

If a single bank were found to have an unusually high proportion of toxic assets, market capital would shift to better-managed banks. If a new bank were created, and found to be efficiently managed, market capital would shift to the new bank and the old ones would fall in value or fail.

What are the advantages of this approach to alternative recapitalization schemes currently under consideration? First, it need not cost the taxpayer a penny. Second, it allows the market to determine asset values. Third, it does not reward bad management but allows bad banks to fail without destroying the entire financial system. Fourth, it provides an incentive for the creation of new financial institutions to replace the old.

The world financial system in 2008 was not illiquid: It was potentially insolvent. This was not a problem of bad fundamentals: It was a problem of market psychology.

In a global financial crisis, there *is* such a thing as a free lunch. When GDP in every country in the world is below potential, and falling, global economic management is not a zero sum game. By preventing a meltdown of the world financial system, we can head off the move to a very bad equilibrium and get the global economy back on track. But to get there, world government leaders and central bankers need to start thinking outside of the box.

MY ARGUMENT SUMMARIZED

Free market economies do not provide the necessary price signals to ensure that a given number of jobs is filled in the right way. Because these signals are missing, a market economy can become stuck with very high unemployment that doesn't go away.

Firms decide how many workers to hire based on the demand for the goods that they produce. The demand for goods depends on wealth, and different levels of wealth lead to different unemployment rates. The wealth of households depends on what other households believe. Wealth depends on confidence!

For every self-fulfilling belief about the value of wealth there is an unemployment rate that will persist for a very long time, and each of these unemployment rates is associated with a different set of prices for houses and a different set of prices for factories and machines. The value of physical assets depends on what market participants think they will be worth in the future.

Fiscal and monetary policy cannot help us to escape from high unemployment unless these policies also restore confidence in the stock market. There is no guarantee that this will happen. In the summer of 2009, many economists were predicting that economic growth would reappear in the United States and in the UK in the third or fourth quarter of the year and that the economy would begin to recover. Nobody was predicting that unemployment would fall any time soon.

It is my view that when world economies emerge from the 2008 crisis, forecasters in every country in the world will revise upward their estimates of their nations' natural rates of unemployment in response to the fact that the world recession has permanently destroyed jobs. Central bankers will be forced to raise domestic interest rates while unemployment is still well above its prerecession rate in order to prevent inflation.

From the perspective of classical and new-Keynesian theory, central bankers will be making the correct decision. They believe that the new higher rates of unemployment that will emerge are permanent features of their domestic economies that are due to changes in economic fundamentals. In a sense, they are right; but the fundamental that has changed is the confidence of stock market participants, and confidence is not independent of policy.

The correct response to the crisis is to set in place, in every country in the world, an institution to control the value of national stock market wealth by targeting the rate of growth of an index fund. Ideally, this function would be taken on by the nation's central bank and coordinated with domestic monetary policy. Central banks should use changes in the size of their balance sheets to prevent inflation from rising too high or too low. They should use changes in the composition of their balance sheets to prevent bubbles and crashes.

BETWEEN KEYNES AND HAYEK

Belief in the market is infectious and, for the most part, it has served us well. In the 1940s, it was by no means clear that the socialist experiment that was tried in the Soviet Union and China would not triumph over capitalism: As late as 1956, Kruschev was able to confidently assert, "We will bury you." In postwar Europe, socialist ideas were in the ascendancy and most intellectuals subscribed to the rationalist idea that a planned society was bound to work better than the anarchy of the market.

A lone voice was that of Friedrich von Hayek, an Austrian-born economist who left his home country to avoid the Nazis. Hayek spent much of his career at the London School of Economics. In 1944, he wrote an important book, *The Road to Serfdom*, in which he argued in defense of free markets based on the idea that a social planner can never have enough knowledge about individual preferences or local conditions to make the right decisions, even if we could all agree on what that means.[1] Hayek was a formative influence on the Reagan and Thatcher revolutions, and his ideas were, arguably, a driving force behind the fall of communism.

FIGURE 11.1 Friedrich A. von Hayek, 1899–1992. Hayek was an economist and philosopher known for his defense of classical liberalism and free market capitalism. He is one of the most important economic and political philosophers of the twentieth century. Along with Gunar Myrdal, he was awarded the Nobel Prize in 1974 "for their pioneering work in the theory of money and economic fluctuations and for their penetrating analysis of the interdependence of economic, social and institutional phenomena." (AP Images)

Hayek and Keynes were friends—although they did not agree about economics. Hayek was a fierce defender of free markets. Keynes believed that it was the role of the intellectual to save the world from communism. In this book, I have tried to walk a tightrope stretched between these two extreme positions. There is much to be admired in the market system. It is the single most powerful engine of economic growth that human beings have devised. But we have not lived in a free market system for at least a century. The question is not whether to regulate the market—it is how to regulate it. As we learn more about market systems perhaps we will understand better not just why they work well but also how they occasionally fail. It is my hope that we can learn to control the economy that we live in without killing the goose that lays the golden egg.

Glossary

Accord: An agreement between the Treasury and the Fed, signed in 1951, that freed the Fed from an obligation to maintain a low interest rate.

Aggregate demand and supply: A theory developed by Keynes to explain GDP and employment. Aggregate demand refers to the factors that determine the money value of expenditures by households, firms, and government on new goods produced in the economy in a given year. Aggregate supply refers to the factors that determine the relationship between the dollar value of GDP and employment. This should not be confused with the theory of demand and supply, which refers to the determinants of price and quantity for a single good.

Animal spirits: The notion that confidence can act as an independent influence on economic activity.

Black Monday: (1) Monday, October 28, 1929, the beginning of the Great Depression. (2) Monday, October 19, 1987, the biggest one-day percentage decline in the stock market in U.S. history.

Bubble: A chain of trades of an asset, each associated with a consecutively higher price, in which each purchase is justified solely by the expectation that the price will move even higher in the future.

Business cycle: The tendency of economic time series to move up and down together in an apparently random, but partly predictable fashion.

Classical economics: The twin doctrines that (1) general equilibrium theory determines quantities traded and relative prices and (2) the quantity theory of money is an accurate description of the determinants of money prices and the rate of inflation.

Classical search theory: See "search theory."

Competitive equilibrium: A set of prices and a set of quantities allocated to each buyer and seller, such that demand and supply are equal in all markets at the same time.

Contraction: See "recession."

Corporate paper: A short-term unsecured loan to a nonfinancial corporation, typically with a duration of less than nine months.

Debt (of government):   The accumulated value of the deficit over many years. The debt is the dollar value of liabilities of the government to the public, both in the United States and abroad.

Deficit (of government):   The excess of the amount that the government spends in a given year over and above the amount it collects in taxes. The deficit is the rate of increase of the debt.

Demand and supply: The theory that determinants of the quantity traded, of a single good, and its price can be divided into two groups: factors that determine demand and those that determine supply. The theory of demand and supply should not be confused with the theory of aggregate demand and aggregate supply, which applies to the economy as a whole.

Depression: A period of diminished economic activity with at least one year where output is 20% below the trend.

Economic model: A mathematical description of an economic theory.

Endowment: The stock of available resources at a point in time. The economy's endowment includes its stock of skilled and unskilled labor and the available stocks of factories, machines, and houses.

Fair value accounting: A regulatory change, introduced in the 1990s, that requires companies to value their assets through mark-to-market procedures. Mark-to-market requires assets to be priced at the value they could be sold at in the current market.

Fiat money: An object valued in exchange solely as a result of a decree by the government that it should be accepted as payment of a debt.

First welfare theorem: The proposition that under certain conditions, a competitive equilibrium is Pareto efficient, in other words, that the free market works well.

Fiscal policy: The choice of the tax rate and the quantity of expenditure by government.

Friction: A cost of trade that prevents the price of a good from adjusting immediately to the point where the quantity demanded and the quantity supplied are equal.

Fundamentals: An underlying determinant of economic activity. Economists typically recognize three fundamentals: preferences, endowments, and technology. Note: Confidence is not a fundamental under standard definitions of the term.

General equilibrium theory: A theory developed by Léon Walras that applies the theory of demand and supply to all markets simultaneously.

Glass-Steagall Act: The name popularly given to the Bank Act, passed in 1933, which created the Federal Deposit Insurance Corporation and separated commercial from investment banking. Many of its provisions were repealed by the Gramm-Leach-Bliley Act of 1999.

Gold standard: A monetary system where each country's currency is convertible to gold at a fixed rate.

Gramm-Leach-Bliley Act: An act of Congress to deregulate financial markets, passed in 1999. It repealed many of the regulations that had been passed in the Glass-Steagall Act of 1933 as a response to the Great Depression.

Great moderation: The observation that output growth, inflation, and the interest rate have all been significantly less volatile in the United States after 1979 than before.

Gross domestic product (GDP):   The money value of all goods and services produced in a country in a given period of time.

Index fund: A mutual fund that consists of a basket of securities whose composition is chosen to track the value of a stock market index.

Inflation: The rate of change of the general level of money prices. The general level of prices is defined by constructing an index of the prices of different goods weighted by their importance. An example is the consumer price index.

Invisible hand: The idea, due to Adam Smith, that free markets allocate resources efficiently.

Liquidity: The ability of an asset to be quickly bought or sold on the market at a value that reflects its long-term value.

Microeconomics: The study of the behavior of individual households and firms and their interaction in markets.

Macroeconomics: The study of the determinants of GDP, employment, interest rates, and prices and how they interact in the economy as a whole.

Match: The act by which a searching worker is paired with a vacant job.

Model: See "economic model."

Monetary policy: The policy of choosing the interest rate that the government will pay on its short-term debt. In the United States, the interest rate is manipulated through open market operations.

Money price: The price of a good in terms of money. For example, the dollar price of a room for one night in a hotel in Hawaii.

Multiplier: The Keynesian theory that a \$1 increase in government expenditure will lead to a more than one dollar increase in aggregate demand.

Natural rate of unemployment: The unemployment rate that would be chosen by a benevolent social planner whose goal was to maximize social welfare. Milton Friedman defined it to be the unemployment rate that would occur in a model of a free market economy that accounts for search frictions. These two definitions are only equivalent if the first welfare theorem holds.

Neutrality of money: The doctrine that, in the long run, the average level of money prices is proportional to the stock of money in an economy.

New-Keynesian economics: A theory that explains why changes in the quantity of money affect the real economy in the short run by postulating the existence of frictions that prevent prices from quickly adjusting to clear markets.

Open market operations: A system for controlling the interest rate, operated by the Fed, through the purchase and sale of Treasury bills in the open market.

Pareto efficiency: A way of allocating commodities in society that cannot be improved upon in a way that everyone would agree to.

Phillips curve: A relationship between the unemployment rate and the rate of change of money wages that was uncovered by A. W. Phillips. It was stable from 1860 to 1950 but disappeared in the 1970s.

Preferences: The factors that determine the tastes of households for one type of good rather than another. Preferences change relatively slowly and are assumed by economists to be fixed in the medium term.

Price index: A weighted average of the prices of a basket of goods.

Quantitative easing: The proposal for a nation's central bank to buy assets other than short-term Treasury bills to expand the money supply.

Quantity theory of money: The theory that the general level of prices is determined, in the long run, by the quantity of money. The quantity theory dates back at least to David Hume in the seventeenth century and was reformulated in recent years by Milton Friedman.

Rational expectations: The theory that beliefs about the future must be consistent, on average, with what happens, in other words, that you can't fool all of the people all of the time.

Rational expectations revolution: The resurgence of general equilibrium theory as an organizing principle for macroeconomics that occurred in the 1970s following the work of Robert E. Lucas Jr. It had two parts: real business cycle theory, which explains real quantities and relative prices, and new-Keynesian economics, which explains how money influences the real economy in the short run and prices in the long run.

Real business cycle theory: The extension of general equilibrium theory from a description of markets at a point in time to a theory of all markets at all points in time. It explains business cycles as efficient responses of the market system to shocks to fundamentals.

Recession: The National Bureau of Economic Research defines a recession (or a contraction) to be a significant decline in economic activity spread across the economy, lasting more than a few months, normally visible in real GDP, real income, employment, industrial production, and wholesale-retail sales. An alternative popular definition is two consecutive quarters of negative GDP growth.

Relative price: The relative quantity of one good that must be given up in exchange for another. For example, the number of hours you would need to work to buy a vacation in Hawaii.

Search technology: A description of the process by which an unemployed worker is matched with a vacant job through the use of time and effort on the part of the unemployed worker and the personnel department of the firm.

Search theory (classical):   The theory that the natural rate of unemployment can be explained by expanding general equilibrium theory to include the costs of looking for a job. These costs are called search frictions.

Self-fulfilling prophecy: A prediction that causes itself to become true. The term was coined by the sociologist Robert K. Merton (1968), and since that date it has been widely applied in the social sciences to understand phenomena where the confidence of market participants independently influences realized events.

Social planner: A fictional character whose goal is to direct the activities of every household and firm in order to maximize social welfare.

Specie: An obsolete term that refers to gold or silver used as money.

Stagflation: The coincidence of high inflation and high unemployment.

Technology: A set of blueprints that define the ways that one set of goods can be transformed into another. Improvements in technology are responsible for economic growth.

Trade-off: The idea that one goal must be sacrificed to achieve another. For example, Samuelson and Solow argued that government must accept higher unemployment to achieve lower inflation.

Notes

Preface

1. The technical details of my argument are explained in *Expectations, Employment and Prices* (2010), a book aimed at Ph.D. economists. Also see my working paper (2009).

Chapter 1

1. Hayek (1944).
2. "The most powerful critique of socialist planning and the socialist state which I read at this time [the late 1940s], and to which I have returned so often since [is] F. A. Hayek's *The Road to Serfdom*." Thatcher (1995, p. 50).
3. Reported on MSNBC Dec. 20, 2006 (http://www.msnbc.msn.com/id/16299324/).
4. See the January 2009 discussion in *Reason Magazine* (http://www.reason.com/news/printer/130348.html).
5. Mackay (1841).
6. Tobin (2008).
7. Barro (2009), Taylor (2009).
8. A self-fulfilling prophecy is a prediction that causes itself to become true. The term was coined by the sociologist Robert K. Merton in 1968, and since that date it has been widely applied in the social sciences to understand phenomena where the confidence of market participants independently influences realized events.

Chapter 2

1. Léon Walras, *Elements of Pure Economics* (1899). *Elements* was published in 1874 in French but was not translated into English until 1954.

2. An earlier statement of the quantity theory can be traced to the seventeenth-century English philosopher John Locke, "Some Considerations of the Lowering of Interest and the Raising the Value of Money." This is a letter sent to a member of Parliament on November 7, 1691. Available online at http://www.marxists. org/reference/subject/economics/locke/part1.htm

3. Marshall's book, *Principles of Economics* (1920, 8th ed.), was published in eight editions and used as a textbook in the teaching of economics for more than 50 years.

4. Skidelsky (1983, p. 11).

5. Skidelsky (1983, p. 40).

6. *The Concise Encyclopedia of Economics* (http://www.econlib.org/ library/CEE.html).

7. The use of coins in medieval Europe is described by Carlo Cipolla, *Money, Prices and Civilization in the Ancient World* (1936).

8. *Of Money* was published in *Political Discourses* in 1752 and reprinted in *Essays: Moral Political and Literary* (1754).

9. The fact that Denis is the *last* worker is important because economists assume that each successive worker adds less to output than the previous one. This idea was introduced into economics in the nineteenth century by William Stanley Jevons, Carl Menger, and Léon Walras.

Chapter 3

1. *A Tract on Monetary Reform* (1924, chapter 3).

2. Pigou (1929).

3. Robert Skidelsky (1992, chapter 14).

4. There appears to be a long history of misattributions of this quote. In private correspondence, Riccardo DiCecio pointed out to me that the phrase "We are all Keynesians now," often attributed to President Nixon, is from Milton Friedman and incomplete. Nixon said, "I'm now a Keynesian in economics," according to journalist Howard K. Smith of ABC News. Friedman in an interview with

Time said, "in one sense, we are all Keynesians now; in another, no one is a Keynesian any longer." However, *Time* magazine only quoted "We are all Keynesians now."

Chapter 4

1. Cochrane (2001).
2. Phillips (1958).
3. This picture is reprinted from Bissell (2007).
4. "Analytical Aspects of Anti-Inflation Policy," *American Economic Review* (1960). Along with Franco Modigliani of MIT and James Tobin of Yale University (both deceased), Paul Samuelson (who died in December 2009) and Robert Solow (an emeritus professor at MIT) have been two of the most influential Keynesian economists.
5. "The Role of Monetary Policy," Friedman (1968); "Money Wage Dynamics and Labor Market Equilibrium," Phelps (1968).
6. But it is possible to find indirect evidence against the natural rate hypothesis. See my 2007 paper with Andreas Beyer of the European Central Bank on this topic. See also the work of Olivier Blanchard and Lawrence Summers (1987) and Brad De Long and Lawrence Summers (1988).
7. Popper made this argument in a celebrated book, *Conjectures and Refutations* (1963).

Chapter 5

1. "Expectations and the Neutrality of Money" (1972). At the time that this paper was published, the dominant view of macro-economists was that macroeconomics describes what happens if prices are too slow to adjust to clear markets. Prominent work in this vein includes Malinvaud (1977), Leijonhufvud (1966), and Barro and Grossman (1971). After the rational expectations revolution, these ideas disappeared from major departments throughout the world.
2. Debreu's monograph *Theory of Value* (1959) provides a rigorous mathematical description of general equilibrium theory. Debreu is one of three economists who made significant developments in general equilibrium theory in the late twentieth century. The other two were Kenneth Arrow of Stanford University and Lionel McKenzie of the University of Rochester.

3. An important article in this vein is "On the Mechanics of Economic Development" (1988), which makes the case that economists should devote their energies to studying growth rather than business cycles.

4. For the adventurous general reader, I recommend the article "Understanding Business Cycles" by Lucas Jr. (1977), which provides a verbal description of equilibrium business cycle theory. This article is extremely clear and does not use mathematics, but it presupposes a knowledge of introductory economics that may make it hard to read for the nonspecialist. The term "Real Business Cycles" was introduced into economics in a 1983 article by two economists, John Long and Charles Plosser (1983). This appeared in print at about the same time as a paper by Finn Kydland and Edward Prescott (1982) with the less appealing title of "Time to Build and Aggregate Fluctuations." It was Long and Plosser's title that stuck.

5. Woodford's book *Interest and Prices* (2003) and Galí's *Monetary Policy, Inflation and the Business Cycle* (2008) provide comprehensive accounts of new-Keynesian economics. Neither book is aimed at the general reader, although Galí's is the more approachable of the two for the nonspecialist. The new-Keynesians provided a theoretical model to account for David Hume's distinction between the short-run and long-run effects of monetary policy. Influential papers in the literature include Mankiw (1985), Akerlof and Yellen (1985), and Calvo (1983), each of which has been used to explain the frictions that prevent prices from adjusting in the classical model.

6. Lucas Jr. (1987). Jordi Galí, Mark Gertler, and Daid Lopéz Salido (2007, p. 56) have shown that a similar calculation applies to the new-Keynesian model.

Chapter 6

1. This situation began to change dramatically in the fall of 2008. Since then the Fed has been expanding the assets that it holds by giving credit to troubled financial institutions and holding a range of lower grade securities as collateral. Between August and December 2008, the Fed's asset position doubled from approximately $850 billion to $1.6 trillion.

2. The gold standard was not fully abandoned until 1971 and, in the period from 1933 to 1971, foreign governments could exchange

dollars for gold at a fixed rate. The period between 1933 and 1971 is known as a gold exchange standard.

3. Robert L. Hetzel and Ralph F. Leach (2001) provide an illuminating discussion of Fed policy during the period immediately following the Accord. Their article describes the role of the Accord in the creation of the modern Fed.

4. Greenspan (2009).

5. The inflation rate is the monthly percentage increase from the same month one year earlier of the Bureau of Labor Statistics Consumer Price Index. The unemployment rate is series LNS14000000 from the Bureau of Labor Statistics.

6. There were three Fed chairmen in the period from 1951 through August 1978. From April 1951 to January 1970, the chair was William McChesney. Martin Jr. Arthur Burns was at the helm from February 1970 to January 1978, and there was a brief interim period from February 1978 to August 1979, when G. William Miller was in charge. The inflation buildup occurred under the tenures of Martin and Burns.

7. Clarida, Galí, and Gertler (2000).

8. Sims and Zha (2006).

9. Woodward (2000, chapter 1).

10. Lucas (1972).

11. Minsky (1975).

Chapter 7

1. Alchian (1970), McCall (1970), Mortensen (1970), Diamond (1982).

2. Shimer (2005). For a modern, although somewhat technical, survey of this literature, see Rogerson, Shimer, and Wright (2005).

3. Notable exceptions that have influenced my own thought include Diamond (1982), Howitt (1986), and Howitt and McAfee (1987), all of whom stress the importance of multiple equilibria.

4. Milton Friedman and Anna Schwartz made the argument in *A Monetary History of the United States* (1963) that the Great Depression was made a great deal worse than it should have been by incompetent monetary policy. For a recent example of a similar argument, see the paper by Harold Cole and Lee Ohanian in the *Journal of Political Economy* (2004). For a criticism of the classical approach to

understanding depressions, see Peter Temin's review article in the *Journal of Economic Literature* (2008).

5. In 2001, the American economists George A. Akerlof, Michael A. Spence, and Joseph E. Stiglitz won the Nobel Prize for their contributions to the theory of markets with asymmetric information.

6. In the first three years of the Great Depression, manufacturing wages rose slightly and real wages increased. Cole and Ohanian (2004).

Chapter 8

1. Wighton (2009).

2. See http://www.aetv.com/flipthishouse/flip2_aboutshow.jsp

3. Robert Shiller (1981) and Steven LeRoy and Richard Porter (1981) made this point in separate articles in 1981.

4. Benhabib and Farmer (1994), Farmer and Guo (1994). The key to understanding how swings in confidence can be rational comes from an important research agenda developed at the University of Pennsylvania in the 1980s. The first paper in this literature is by Karl Shell (1977). Some of the other economists who worked on this idea at Penn in the 1980s include Costas Azariadis (1981), David Cass and Karl Shell (1983), and Roger Farmer and Michael Woodford (1984).

5. For a comparison of my approach to that of Akerlof and Shiller, see my review in the *Economic Record*, (2009). The behaviorist critique of rational man is not new, nor, in my view, is it likely to lead to advances in economics. As David Levine (2009, p. 1) points out in his Max Weber lecture,

> Criticism of homo economicus is not a new topic. In 1898 Thorstein Veblen wrote sarcastically [of] rational economic man as "a lightning calculator of pleasures and pains, who oscillates like a homogenous globule of desire of happiness under the impulse of stimuli." This description had little to do with economics as it was practiced then—and even less now. Indeed, for a long period of time during the 60s and 70s, irrational economic man dominated economics. The much criticized theory of rational expectations was a reaction to the fact that irrational economic man is a no better description of us than that of a "lightning calculator of pleasures and pains." In many ways the rational expectations model was a reaction

to "[t]he implicit presumption in these ... models [of the 60s and 70s] ... that people could be fooled over and over again."

Levine goes on to show that in most cases, conventional economic theory does a much better job of explaining experimental evidence that supposedly overturns homo economicus than is often understood.

6. In Akerlof and Shiller's words (2009, p.26), "capitalism ... does not automatically produce what people really need; it produces what they think they need. ... "

7. See, for example, Friedman's (1957) book, *A Theory of the Consumption Function*, where he introduces the idea of permanent income. Other prominent economists who worked on consumption at this time include James Duesenberry, and Albert Ando and Franco Modigliani.

Chapter 9

1. Kehoe and Prescott (2007). Tim Kehoe is a professor of economics at the University of Minnesota and a leading figure in the revival of general equilibrium theory.

2. Shiller's historical series of house prices since 1890 is available at http://www.econ.yale.edu/~shiller/data.htm.

3. *Wall Street Journal*, October 2, 2008.

4. Nobel Laureate Joseph Stiglitz made this argument in testimony to the House Finanical Services Committee, October 21, 2008.

5. Testimony of Thomas Hamilton, Securities and Financial Markets Association, to the House Committee on Financial Service, May 22, 2008.

Chapter 10

1. This phrase was first used in 1935 by the then Federal Reserve chairman, Marriner Eccles, in congressional hearings on the Banking Act of 1935:

Governor Eccles: Under present circumstances, there is very little, if any, that can be done.

Congressman Goldsborough: You mean you cannot push on a string.

> Governor Eccles: That is a very good way to put it, one cannot push on a string. We are in the depths of a depression and ... beyond creating an easy money situation through reduction of discount rates, there is very little, if anything, that the reserve organization can do to bring about recovery. [U. S. Congress House Banking Currency Committee (1935, p. 377) cited by Wood (2006, p. 231)]

2. Christina D. Romer (February 27, 2009). The Case for Fiscal Stimulus: The Likely Effects of the American Recovery and Reinvestment Act. Available online at http://news.uchicago.edu/files/newsrelease_20090227.pdf

3. The multiplier is supposed to work as follows. Every dollar spent by government increases employment in those industries that produce the goods the government demands. The newly employed workers spend some fraction of their increased income on goods and services, and these increases generate additional employment. The additional employment generates further expenditure, and a cascade of additional expenditures converges to a final increase in aggregate demand that is larger than the initial increase in government purchases by a multiple that depends on the fraction of every extra dollar of income that is saved. It is the success of this theory in influencing politicians that accounts for a vastly increased role of government in the postwar economy.

4. I have divided all dollar figures by a measure of the money wage to remove the influence of real growth and inflation, and I have further divided these numbers by the size of the labor force to put them in per capita terms.

Chapter 11

1. Hayek (1944).

Bibliography

Akerlof, G., and J. Yellen (1985): "A Near Rational Model of the Business Cycle with Wage and Price Inertia," *Quarterly Journal of Economics*, 100, 823–838.

Akerlof, G. A., and R. J. Shiller (2009): *Animal Spirits*. Princeton University Press, Princeton and Oxford.

Alchian, A. A. (1970): "Information Costs, Pricing, and Resource Unemployment," in *Microeconomic Foundations of Employment and Inflation Theory*, ed. by E. S. Phelps. Norton, New York.

Azariadis, C. (1981): "Self-fulfilling Prophecies," *Journal of Economic Theorey*, 25(3), 380–396.

Barro, R. J. (2009): "Government Spending Is No Free Lunch," *Wall Street Journal*, January 22, p. A17.

Barro, R. J., and H. Grossman (1971): "A General Disequilibrium Model of Income and Employment," *American Economic Review*, 61, 82–93.

Benhabib, J., and R. E. A. Farmer (1994): "Indeterminacy and Increasing Returns," *Journal of Economic Theory*, 63, 19–46.

Bernanke, B. S. (May 31, 2003): "Some Thoughts on Monetary Policy in Japan," Remarks Made Before the Japan Society of Monetary Economics.

——— (February 20, 2004): "The Great Moderation," Remarks at the Meeting of the Easten Economics Association, Washington, D.C.

Beyer, A., and R. E. A. Farmer (2007): "Natural Rate Doubts," *Journal of Economic Dynamics and Control*, 31, 797–825.

Bissell, C. (2007): "The Moniac: A Hydromechanical Analog Computer of the 1950s," *IEEE Control Systems Magazine*, 27(1), 69–74.

Blanchard, O. J., and L. H. Summers (1987): "Hysterisis in Unemployment," *European Economic Review*, 31, 288–295.

Calvo, G. A. (1983): "Staggered Prices in a Utility Maximizing Model," *Journal of Monetary Economics*, 12(November), 383–398.

Cass, D., and K. Shell (1983): "Do Sunspots Matter?" *Journal of Political Economy*, 91, 193–227.

Chari, V. V. (1998): "Nobel Laureate Robert E. Lucas, Jr.: Architect of Modern Macroeconomics," *Journal of Economic Perspectives*, 12(1), 171–186.

Cipolla, C. M. (1936): *Money, Prices and Civilization in the Ancient World*. Princeton University Press, Princeton.

Clarida, R., J. Galí, and M. Gertler (2000): "Monetary Policy Rules and Macroeconomic Stability: Evidence and Some Theory," *Quarterly Journal of Economics*, 115(1), 147–180.

Cochrane, J. (2001): *Asset Pricing*. Princeton University Press, Princeton and Oxford.

——— (March 18, 2009): "This House Believes That We Are All Keynesians Now," The Economist Debate Online (http://economist/debate/days/view/283).

Cole, H. L., and L. E. Ohanian (2004): "New Deal Policies and the Persistence of the Great Depression: A General Equilibrium Analysis," *Journal of Political Economy*, 112(4), 779–816.

De Long, B., and L. H. Summers (1988): "How Does Macroeconomic Policy Matter," *Brookings Papers on Economic Activity*, 2, 433–480.

Debreu, G. (1959): *Theory of Value*. Yale University Press, New Haven, CT.

Diamond, P. A. (1982): "Aggregate Demand Management in Search Equilibrium," *Journal of Political Economy*, 90, 881–894.

Farmer, R. E. A. (1993): *The Macroeconomics of Self-Fulfilling Prophecies*, second edition 1999. MIT Press, Cambridge, MA.

——— (2009): "Confidence, Crashes and Animal Spirits," *NBER WP no. 14846*.

——— (2010): *Expectations, Employment and Prices*. Oxford University Press, New York.

——— (2009): "Animal Spirits: How Human Psychology Drives the Economy, and Why It Matters for Global Capitalism, by George A.

Akerlof and Robert J. Shiller. A Review," *The Economic Record*, 85(270), 357–369.

Farmer, R. E. A., and J. T. Guo (1994): "Real Business Cycles and the Animal Spirits Hypothesis," *Journal of Economic Theory*, 63, 42–73.

Farmer, R. E. A., and M. Woodford (1984): "Self-fulfilling Prophecies and the Business Cycle," *Caress Working Paper 84–12.*

Friedman, M. (1957): *A Theory of the Consumption Function.* Princeton University Press, Princeton.

———— (1968): "The Role of Monetary Policy," *American Economic Review*, 58(March), 1–17.

———— (1994): *Money Mischief.* Harcourt Trade, New York.

Friedman, M., and A. J. Schwartz (1963): *A Monetary History of the United States, 1867–1960.* Princeton University Press, Princeton.

Galí, J. (2008): *Monetary Policy, Inflation and the Business Cycle.* Princeton University Press, Princeton.

Galí, J., M. Gertler, and D. L. Salido (2007): "Markups, Gaps and the Welfare Costs of Business Cycle Fluctuations," *Review of Economics and Statistics*, 89(1), 44–59.

Greenspan, A. (June 26, 2009): "Inflation—The Real Threat to a Sustained Recovery," *Financial Times* Economists' Forum (http://blogs.ft.com/economistsforum/2009/06/inflation-the–real-threat-to-sustained-recovery/#more-1046).

Hayek, F. V. (1944): *The Road to Serfdom*, reprint 1972. University of Chicago Press, Chicago.

Hetzel, R. L., and R. F. Leach (2001): "The Treasury-Fed Accord: A New Narrative Account," *Federal Reserve Bank of Richmond Economic Quarterly*, 87(1), 33–55.

Hoover, H. (October 1932): "Address at Madison Square Garden in New York City."

Howitt, P. (1986): "The Keynesian Recovery," *The Canadian Journal of Economics*, 19(4), 626–641.

Howitt, P., and R. P. McAfee (1987): "Costly Search and Recruiting," *International Economic Review*, 28(1), 89–107.

Hume, D. (1754): *Essays: Moral Political and Literary*, 1985. Liberty Fund edition. Liberty Fund, Inc., Indianapolis, IN.

Kehoe, T. J., and E. C. Prescott (2007): *Great Depressions of the Twentieth Century.* Federal Reserve Bank of Minneapolis, Minneapolis, MN.

Keynes, J. M. (1924): *A Tract on Monetary Reform.* Macmillan, London.

Keynes, J. M. (1931): *Essays in Persuasion*, 1963 Norton Library reprint. W. W. Norton and Co., New York.

———(1936): *The General Theory of Employment Interest and Money*. MacMillan, London.

Krugman, P. (January 19, 2009): "Economists, Ideology and Stimulus," *The Conscience of Liberal: New York Times* Blog (http://krugman. blogsmytimes.com/2009/01/19/economists-ideology-and-stimulus).

Kydland, F. E., and E. C. Prescott (1982): "Time to Build and Aggregate Fluctuations," *Econometrica*, 50, 1345–1370.

Leijonhufvud, A. (1966): *On Keynesian Economics and the Economics of Keynes*. Oxford University Press, London.

LeRoy, S., and R. Porter (1981): "Stock Price Volatility: A Test Based on Implied Variance Bounds," *Econometrica*, 49, 97–113.

Levine, D. K. (2009): "Is Behavioral Economics Doomed?: The Ordinary versus the Extraordinary," *Mimeo: Max Weber Lecture*, European University Institute, Florence, Italy.

Long, J. B. J., and C. I. Plosser (1983): "Real Business Cycles," *Journal of Political Economy*, 91(1), 39–69.

Lucas Jr., R. E. (1972): "Expectations and the Neutrality of Money," *Journal of Economic Theory*, 4, 103–124.

———(1977): "Understanding Business Cycles," *Carnegie-Rochester Conference Series on Public Policy*, 5, 7–29.

———(1987): *Models of Business Cycles*. Basil Blackwell, Oxford, UK.

———(1988): "On the Mechanics of Economic Development," *Journal of Monetary Economics*, 22(July), 3–42.

Mackay, C. (1841): *Extraordinary Popular Delusions and the Madness of Crowds*, reprinted 1980. Harmony Books, New York.

Malinvaud, E. (1977): *The Theory of Unemployment Reconsidered*. Basil Blackwell, Oxford, UK.

Mankiw, G. N. (1985): "Small Menu Costs and Large Business Cycles: A Macroeconomic Model of Monopoly," *Quarterly Journal of Economics*, 100, 529–537.

Marshall, A. (1920, 8th ed.): *Principles of Economics*. MacMillan, London.

McCall, J. J. (1970): "Economics of Information and Job Search," *Quarterly Journal of Economics*, 84, 113–126.

Merton, R. K. (1968): *Social Theory and Social Structure*. Free Press, New York.

Mill, J. S. (1824): *Autobigraphy, reprint 2006.* Liberty Fund Inc., Indianapolis, IN.

Minsky, H. P. (1975): *John Maynard Keynes.* Columbia University Press, New York.

Mortensen, D. T. (1970): "Job Search, the Duration of Unemployment, and the Phillips Curve," *American Economic Review*, 60(5), 847–862.

Phelps, E. S. (1968): "Money Wage Dynamics and Labor Market Equilibrium," *Journal of Political Economy*, 76(4), 678–711.

———— (1970): *Microeconomic Foundations of Employment and Inflation Theory.* Norton, New York.

Phillips, A. W. (1958): "The Relationship between Unemployment and the Rate of Change of Money Wages in the United Kingdom 1861–1957," *Economica*, 25(100), 283–299.

Pigou, A. C. (1929): *Industrial Fluctuations.* MacMillan, London.

———— (1933): *The Economics of Welfare.* MacMillan, London.

Pissarides, C. (1990): *Equilibrium Unemployment Theory.* Basil Blackwell, Oxford.

Popper, K. (1963): *Conjectures and Refutations: The Growth of Scientific Knowledge.* Routledge, London.

Rogerson, R., R. Shimer, and R. Wright (2005): "Search-Theoretic Models of the Labor Market: A Survey," *Journal of Economic Literature*, 43, 959–988.

Samuelson, P. A., and R. M. Solow (1960): "Analytical Aspects of Anti-Inflation Policy," *American Economic Review*, 50(2), 177–194.

Shell, K. (1977): "Monnaie et Allocation Intertemporelle," *Mimeo: Malinvaud Seminar, CNRS Paris.*

Shiller, R. J. (1981): "Do Stock Prices Move Too Much to Be Justified by Subsequent Changes in Dividends?" *American Economic Review*, 71, 421–436.

Shimer, R. (2005): "The Cyclical Behavior of Equilibrium Unemployment and Vacancies," *American Economic Review*, 95(1), 25–49.

Sims, C. A., and T. Zha (2006): "Were There Regime Switches in US Monetary Policy?" *American Economic Review*, 96(1), 54–81.

Skidelsky, R. (1983): *John Maynard Keynes: Hopes Betrayed, 1883–1920*, vol. 1. Viking, New York.

———— (1992): *John Maynard Keynes: The Economist as Savior, 1920–1937*, vol. 2. Allen Lane, Penguin Press, London.

Smith, A. (1776): *An Inquiry into the Nature and Causes of the Wealth of Nations*. University of Chicago, Chicago.

Soros, G. (October 10, 2008): Transcript of an Interview: Bill Moyer's Journal. http://www.pbs.org/moyes/journal/10102008/transcript4.html

Steinbeck, J. (1939): *The Grapes of Wrath*, Viking, New York.

Taylor, J. (February 9, 2009): "How Government Created the Financial Crisis," *Wall Street Journal*, p. A19.

Temin, P. (2008): "Real Business Cycle Views of the Great Depression and Recent Events: A Review of Timothy J. Kehoe and Edward C. Prescott's Great Depressions of the Twentieth Century," *Journal of Economic Literature*, 669–684.

Thaler, R. H., and C. R. Sunstein (2009): *Nudge: Improving Decisions about Health, Wealth and Happiness*. Penguin, London.

Thatcher, M. (1995): *The Path to Power*. HarperCollins, New York.

The Concise Encyclopedia of Economics (2009): "Biography of Pareto," Library of Economics and Liberty (http://www.econlib.com/library/Enc/bios/Pareto.html).

Tobin, J. (2008): "Fisher, Irving (1867–1947)," in *The New Palgrave Dictionary of Economics*, ed. by S. N. Durlauf and L. E. Blume. Palgrave Macmillan, Basingstoke.

U. S. Congress House Banking Currency Committee (1935): *Banking Act Hearings of 1935*. Congress of the United States.

Walras, L. (1899): *Elements of Pure Economics*. 4th ed. 1926, rev ed. 1926, Engl transl. 2003. Routledge, New York.

Wighton, D. (January 29, 2009): "Efficient Market Hypothesis Is Dead—For Now," Online Blog (http://business.timesonline.co.uk/tol/business/columnists/article5607960.ece).

Wood, J. H. (2006): *A History of Central Banking in the United States*. Cambridge University Press.

Woodford, M. (2003): *Interest and Prices: Foundations of a Theory of Monetary Policy*. Princeton University Press, Princeton.

Woodward, B. (2000): *Maestro: Greenspan's Fed and the American Boom*. Simon & Schuster, New York.

Index